D1579766

Parish Mass Book

Edited by Kevin Mayhew

OUR LADY OF GRACE AND ST EDWARD CHURCH OF CHISWICK

MAYHEW-McCRIMMON
Great Wakering Essex

First published in Great Britain in 1976 by
MAYHEW-McCRIMMON LTD
Great Wakering Essex

Compilation and layout
© Copyright 1976 by Mayhew-McCrimmon Ltd.

Cum originali concordat
Nihil obstat
Imprimatur
Brentwood, August 28 1976
ISBN 0-85597-170-3

John P. Dewis
Brian O'Higgins, D.D.
Christopher Creede, Vic. Gen.

Acknowledgements

English translation of the Roman Missal copyright © 1973, and 1974, International Committee on English in the Liturgy, Inc. All rights reserved.
The alternative translations of the Antiphons and Prayers are © copyright by the National Liturgical Commission for England and Wales.
The scripture texts are taken from the Jerusalem Bible Version of the Scriptures, copyrighted © in 1966, 1967 and 1968 by Darton, Longman and Todd Ltd. and Doubleday and Co. Inc., and used by permission.
The version of the Psalms is that translated from the Hebrew by the Grail, copyright © 1963, The Grail (England) and published by William Collins and Sons Ltd in The Psalms: A New Translation. Used by permission.

Printed by Silver End Press, London and Essex.

Contents

The Order of Mass

When the people have assembled the priest goes to the altar. If there is no hymn Turn to the Proper of the Day *for the Entrance Antiphon. Then everyone makes the sign of the cross as the priest says:*

In the name of the Father, and of the Son, and of the Holy Spirit.
Amen.

The priest greets the people in one of the following ways, or in similar words:

1 The grace of our Lord Jesus Christ and the love of God
   and the fellowship of the Holy Spirit be with you all.
   And also with you.

2 The grace and peace of God our Father and the Lord Jesus Christ be with you.
   Blessed be God, the Father of our Lord Jesus Christ. *or* **And also with you.**

3 The Lord be with you.
   And also with you.

The priest invites the people to repentance in one of the following ways, or in similar words:

1 My brothers and sisters,
   to prepare ourselves to celebrate the sacred mysteries,
   let us call to mind our sins.

After a brief silence, all say:

I confess to almighty God,
and to you, my brothers and sisters,
that I have sinned through my own fault

All strike their breast

in my thoughts and in my words
in what I have done,
and in what I have failed to do;
and I ask blessed Mary, ever virgin,
all the angels and saints,
and you, my brothers and sisters,
to pray for me to the Lord our God.

May almighty God have mercy on us,
forgive us our sins,
and bring us to everlasting life.
Amen.

Lord, have mercy. **Lord, have mercy.**
Christ, have mercy. **Christ, have mercy.**
Lord, have mercy. **Lord, have mercy.**
Turn to the Gloria on page 6 except during Advent and Lent.

---

2 My brothers and sisters,
    to prepare ourselves to celebrate the sacred mysteries,
    let us call to mind our sins.

After a brief silence, the celebrant says:

Lord, we have sinned against you:
Lord, have mercy.
Lord, have mercy.
Lord, show us your mercy and love.
And grant us your salvation.
May almighty God have mercy on us,
forgive us our sins,
and bring us to everlasting life.
Amen.
Lord, have mercy. **Lord, have mercy.**
Christ, have mercy. **Christ, have mercy.**
Lord, have mercy. **Lord, have mercy.**
Turn to the Gloria on page 6 except during Advent and Lent.

---

3 My brothers and sisters,
    to prepare ourselves to celebrate the sacred mysteries,
    let us call to mind our sins.

After a brief silence the priest says the following, or uses similar words. The people's response, however, remains the same.

You were sent to heal the contrite:
Lord, have mercy.
Lord, have mercy.
You came to call sinners:
Christ, have mercy.
Christ, have mercy.
You plead for us at the right hand of the Father:
Lord, have mercy.
Lord, have mercy.
May almighty God have mercy on us,
forgive us our sins,
and bring us to everlasting life.
Amen.

THE GLORIA

Glory to God in the highest,
   and peace to his people on earth.

Lord God, heavenly King,
almighty God and Father,
   we worship you, we give you thanks,
   we praise you for your glory.

Lord Jesus Christ, only Son of the Father,
Lord God, Lamb of God,
you take away the sin of the world:
   have mercy on us;
you are seated at the right hand of the Father:
   receive our prayer.

For you alone are the Holy One,
you alone are the Lord,
you alone are the Most High,
   Jesus Christ,
   with the Holy Spirit,
   in the glory of God the Father. Amen.

Now Turn to the Proper of the Day *for the Opening Prayer and the Readings.*

CREED

We believe in one God,
   the Father, the Almighty,
   maker of heaven and earth,
   of all that is, seen and unseen.

We believe in one Lord, Jesus Christ,
   the only Son of God,
   eternally begotten of the Father,
   God from God, Light from Light,
   true God from true God,
   begotten, not made,
   of one Being with the Father.
   Through him all things were made.
   For us men and for our salvation
      he came down from heaven: *all bow*
   by the power of the Holy Spirit
      he became incarnate from the Virgin Mary, and was made man.

For our sake he was crucified under Pontius Pilate;
   he suffered death and was buried.
   On the third day he rose again
      in accordance with the Scriptures;
   he ascended into heaven
      and is seated at the right hand of the Father.
He will come again in glory to judge the living and the dead,
   and his kingdom will have no end.

We believe in the Holy Spirit, the Lord, the giver of life,
who proceeds from the Father and the Son.
With the Father and the Son he is worshipped and glorified.
He has spoken through the Prophets.
We believe in one holy catholic and apostolic Church.
We acknowledge one baptism for the forgiveness of sins.
We look for the resurrection of the dead,
and the life of the world to come. Amen.

THE PRAYER OF THE FAITHFUL

After an invitation, there follows a series of petitions to which the people answer **Lord,
graciously hear us** *or any other customary response. A prayer by the priest concludes
and all answer* **Amen.**

THE OFFERING

*During the offertory the offerings are brought to the altar and the people may sing a
hymn while the priest says quietly the following prayers. If there is no hymn the people
make the responses given here to the prayer of offering.*

Blessed are you, Lord, God of all creation.
Through your goodness we have this bread to offer,
which earth has given and human hands have made.
It will become for us the bread of life.
Blessed be God for ever.

By the mystery of this water and wine may we come to share in the divinity of Christ,
who humbled himself to share in our humanity.

Blessed are you, Lord, God of all creation.
Through your goodness we have this wine to offer,
fruit of the vine and work of human hands.
It will become our spiritual drink.
Blessed be God for ever.

Lord God, we ask you to receive us and be pleased with the sacrifice we offer you
with humble and contrite hearts.

The priest washes his hands, saying quietly:

Lord, wash away my iniquity;
cleanse me from my sin.

Pray, brethren, that my sacrifice and yours
may be acceptable to God the almighty Father.
**May the Lord accept the sacrifice at your hands,
for the praise and glory of his name,
for our good, and the good of all his Church.**

Now Turn to the Proper of the Day *for the Prayer Over the Gifts.*

THE PREFACE (General Use)

The Lord be with you.
And also with you.
Lift up your hearts.
We lift them up to the Lord.
Let us give thanks to the Lord our God.
It is right to give him thanks and praise.

A Preface to the Eucharistic Prayer follows. At the end of the Preface everyone says or sings:

Holy, holy, holy Lord, God of power and might, heaven and earth are full of your glory.
   Hosanna in the highest.

Blessed is he who comes in the name of the Lord.
   Hosanna in the highest.

Turn to
page 15 for Eucharistic Prayer 1
page 18 for Eucharistic Prayer 2
page 20 for Eucharistic Prayer 3
page 22 for Eucharistic Prayer 4

ADVENT 1 (1st Sunday of Advent – December 16)

The Lord be with you.
And also with you.
Lift up your hearts.
We lift them up to the Lord.
Let us give thanks to the Lord our God.
It is right to give him thanks and praise.

Father, all-powerful and ever-living God,
we do well always and everywhere to give you thanks
through Jesus Christ our Lord.

When he humbled himself to come among us as a man,
he fulfilled the plan you formed long ago
and opened for us the way to salvation.

Now we watch for the day,
hoping that the salvation promised us will be ours
when Christ our Lord will come again in his glory.

And so, with all the choirs of angels in heaven
we proclaim your glory
and join in their unending hymn of praise:

Holy, holy, holy Lord, God of power and might, heaven and earth are full of your glory.
   Hosanna in the highest.

Blessed is he who comes in the name of the Lord.
   Hosanna in the highest.

Turn to
page 15 for Eucharistic Prayer 1
page 18 for Eucharistic Prayer 2
page 20 for Eucharistic Prayer 3
page 22 for Eucharistic Prayer 4

ADVENT 2 (December 17–December 24)

The Lord be with you. **And also with you.**

Lift up your hearts. **We lift them up to the Lord.**

Let us give thanks to the Lord our God. **It is right to give him thanks and praise.**

Father, all-powerful and ever-living God,
we do well always and everywhere to give you thanks
through Jesus Christ our Lord.
His future coming was proclaimed by all the prophets.
The virgin mother bore him in her womb
    with love beyond all telling.
John the Baptist was his herald
and made him known when at last he came.
In his love Christ has filled us with joy
as we prepare to celebrate his birth,
so that when he comes he may find us watching in prayer,
our hearts filled with wonder and praise.
And so, with all the choirs of angels in heaven
we proclaim your glory
and join in their unending hymn of praise:

Holy, holy, holy Lord, God of power and might,
heaven and earth are full of your glory.
    Hosanna in the highest.
Blessed is he who comes in the name of the Lord.
    Hosanna in the highest.

Turn to
page 15 for Eucharistic Prayer 1
page 18 for Eucharistic Prayer 2
page 20 for Eucharistic Prayer 3
page 22 for Eucharistic Prayer 4

CHRISTMAS 1

The Lord be with you. **And also with you.**

Lift up your hearts. **We lift them up to the Lord.**

Let us give thanks to the Lord our God. **It is right to give him thanks and praise.**

Father, all-powerful and ever-living God,
we do well always and everywhere to give you thanks
through Jesus Christ our Lord.
In the wonder of the incarnation
your eternal Word has brought to the eyes of faith
a new and radiant vision of your glory.
In him we see our God made visible
and so are caught up in love of the God we cannot see.
And so, with all the choirs of angels in heaven
we proclaim your glory
and join in their unending hymn of praise:

Holy, holy, holy Lord, God of power and might,
heaven and earth are full of your glory.
    Hosanna in the highest.
Blessed is he who comes in the name of the Lord.
    Hosanna in the highest.

Turn to
page 15 for Eucharistic Prayer 1
page 18 for Eucharistic Prayer 2
page 20 for Eucharistic Prayer 3
page 22 for Eucharistic Prayer 4

THE EPIPHANY

The Lord be with you.	**And also with you.**
Lift up your hearts.	**We lift them up to the Lord.**
Let us give thanks to the Lord our God.	**It is right to give him thanks and praise.**

Father, all-powerful and ever-living God,
we do well always and everywhere to give you thanks.

Today you revealed in Christ your eternal plan of salvation
and showed him as the light of all peoples.
Now that his glory has shone among us
you have renewed humanity in his immortal image.

Now, with angels and archangels,
and the whole company of heaven,
we sing the unending hymn of your praise:

Holy, holy, holy Lord, God of power and might,
heaven and earth are full of your glory.
> **Hosanna in the highest.**

Blessed is he who comes in the name of the Lord.
> **Hosanna in the highest.**

Turn to
page 15 for Eucharistic Prayer 1
page 18 for Eucharistic Prayer 2
page 20 for Eucharistic Prayer 3
page 22 for Eucharistic Prayer 4

SUNDAYS OF THE YEAR 1

The Lord be with you.	**And also with you.**
Lift up your hearts.	**We lift them up to the Lord.**
Let us give thanks to the Lord our God.	**It is right to give him thanks and praise.**

Father, all-powerful and ever-living God,
we do well always and everywhere to give you thanks
through Jesus Christ our Lord.

Through his cross and resurrection
he freed us from sin and death
and called us to the glory that has made us
a chosen race, a royal priesthood,
a holy nation, a people set apart.

Everywhere we proclaim your mighty works
for you have called us out of darkness
into your own wonderful light.

And so, with all the choirs of angels in heaven
we proclaim your glory
and join in their unending hymn of praise:

Holy, holy, holy Lord, God of power and might,
heaven and earth are full of your glory.
> **Hosanna in the highest.**

Blessed is he who comes in the name of the Lord.
> **Hosanna in the highest.**

Turn to
page 15 for Eucharistic Prayer 1
page 18 for Eucharistic Prayer 2
page 20 for Eucharistic Prayer 3
page 22 for Eucharistic Prayer 4

SUNDAYS OF THE YEAR 2

The Lord be with you.	**And also with you.**
Lift up your hearts.	**We lift them up to the Lord.**
Let us give thanks to the Lord our God.	**It is right to give him thanks and praise.**

Father, all-powerful and ever-living God,
we do well always and everywhere to give you thanks
through Jesus Christ our Lord.

Out of love for sinful man,
he humbled himself to be born of the Virgin.

By suffering on the cross
he freed us from unending death,
and by rising from the dead
he gave us eternal life.

And so, with all the choirs of angels in heaven
we proclaim your glory
and join in their unending hymn of praise:

Holy, holy, holy Lord, God of power and might,
heaven and earth are full of your glory.
   Hosanna in the highest.

Blessed is he who comes in the name of the Lord.
   Hosanna in the highest.

Turn to
page 15 for Eucharistic Prayer 1
page 18 for Eucharistic Prayer 2
page 20 for Eucharistic Prayer 3
page 22 for Eucharistic Prayer 4

SUNDAYS OF THE YEAR 5

The Lord be with you.	**And also with you.**
Lift up your hearts.	**We lift them up to the Lord.**
Let us give thanks to the Lord our God.	**It is right to give him thanks and praise.**

Father, all-powerful and ever-living God,
we do well always and everywhere to give you thanks.

All things are of your making,
all times and seasons obey your laws,
but you chose to create man in your own image,
setting him over the whole world in all its wonder.
You made man the steward of creation,
to praise you day by day for the marvels of your wisdom and
   power,
through Jesus Christ our Lord.

We praise you, Lord, with all the angels
in their song of joy:

Holy, holy, holy Lord, God of power and might,
heaven and earth are full of your glory.
   Hosanna in the highest.

Blessed is he who comes in the name of the Lord.
   Hosanna in the highest.

Turn to
page 15 for Eucharistic Prayer 1
page 18 for Eucharistic Prayer 2
page 20 for Eucharistic Prayer 3
page 22 for Eucharistic Prayer 4

12

LENT 1

The Lord be with you.	**And also with you.**
Lift up your hearts.	**We lift them up to the Lord.**
Let us give thanks to the Lord our God.	**It is right to give him thanks and praise.**

Father, all-powerful and ever-living God,
we do well always and everywhere to give you thanks
through Jesus Christ our Lord.

Each year you give us this joyful season
when we prepare to celebrate the paschal mystery
with mind and heart renewed.
You give us a spirit of loving reverence for you, our Father,
and of willing service to our neighbour.

As we recall the great events that gave us a new life in Christ,
you bring the image of your Son to perfection within us.

Now, with angels and archangels,
and the whole company of heaven,
we sing the unending hymn of praise:

Holy, holy, holy Lord, God of power and might,
heaven and earth are full of your glory.
   Hosanna in the highest.

Blessed is he who comes in the name of the Lord.
   Hosanna in the highest.

Turn to
page 15 for Eucharistic Prayer 1
page 18 for Eucharistic Prayer 2
page 20 for Eucharistic Prayer 3
page 22 for Eucharistic Prayer 4

LENT 2

The Lord be with you.	**And also with you.**
Lift up your hearts.	**We lift them up to the Lord.**
Let us give thanks to the Lord our God.	**It is right to give him thanks and praise.**

Father, all-powerful and ever-living God,
we do well always and everywhere to give you thanks.

This great season of grace is your gift to your family
to renew us in spirit.
You give us strength to purify our hearts,
to control our desires,
and so to serve you in freedom.
You teach us how to live in this passing world,
with our heart set on the world that will never end.

Now, with all the saints and angels,
we praise you for ever:

Holy, holy, holy Lord, God of power and might,
heaven and earth are full of your glory.
   Hosanna in the highest.

Blessed is he who comes in the name of the Lord.
   Hosanna in the highest.

Turn to
page 15 for Eucharistic Prayer 1
page 18 for Eucharistic Prayer 2
page 20 for Eucharistic Prayer 3
page 22 for Eucharistic Prayer 4

PASSION SUNDAY

The Lord be with you.	**And also with you.**
Lift up your hearts.	**We lift them up to the Lord.**
Let us give thanks to the Lord our God.	**It is right to give him thanks and praise.**

Father, all-powerful and ever-living God,
we do well always and everywhere to give you thanks
through Jesus Christ our Lord.
Though he was sinless, he suffered willingly for sinners.
Though innocent, he accepted death to save the guilty.
By his dying he has destroyed our sins.
By his rising he has raised us up to holiness of life.
We praise you, Lord, with all the angels
in their song of joy:

**Holy, holy, holy Lord, God of power and might,
heaven and earth are full of your glory.**
  Hosanna in the highest.
Blessed is he who comes in the name of the Lord.
  Hosanna in the highest.

*Turn to
page 15 for Eucharistic Prayer 1
page 18 for Eucharistic Prayer 2
page 20 for Eucharistic Prayer 3
page 22 for Eucharistic Prayer 4*

HOLY THURSDAY

The Lord be with you.	**And also with you.**
Lift up your hearts.	**We lift them up to the Lord.**
Let us give thanks to the Lord our God.	**It is right to give him thanks and praise.**

Father, all-powerful and ever-living God,
we do well always and everywhere to give you thanks
through Jesus Christ our Lord.
He is the true and eternal priest
who established this unending sacrifice.
He offered himself as a victim for our deliverance
and taught us to make this offering in his memory.
As we eat his body which he gave for us,
we grow in strength.
As we drink his blood which he poured out for us,
we are washed clean.
Now, with angels and archangles,
and the whole company of heaven,
we sing the unending hymn of your praise:

**Holy, holy, holy Lord, God of power and might,
heaven and earth are full of your glory.**
  Hosanna in the highest.
Blessed is he who comes in the name of the Lord.
  Hosanna in the highest.

*Turn to
page 15 for Eucharistic Prayer 1
page 18 for Eucharistic Prayer 2
page 20 for Eucharistic Prayer 3
page 22 for Eucharistic Prayer 4*

EASTER 1

The Lord be with you.	**And also with you.**
Lift up your hearts.	**We lift them up to the Lord.**
Let us give thanks to the Lord our God.	**It is right to give him thanks and praise.**

Father, all-powerful and ever-living God,
we do well always and everywhere to give you thanks
through Jesus Christ our Lord.

We praise you with greater joy than ever
on this Easter night (day),
when Christ became our paschal sacrifice.

He is the true Lamb who took away the sins of the world.
By dying he destroyed our death;
by rising he restored our life.

And so, with all the choirs of angels in heaven
we proclaim your glory
and join in their unending hymn of praise:

Holy, holy, holy Lord, God of power and might,
heaven and earth are full of your glory.
  Hosanna in the highest.

Blessed is he who comes in the name of the Lord.
  Hosanna in the highest.

Turn to
page 15 for Eucharistic Prayer 1
page 18 for Eucharistic Prayer 2
page 20 for Eucharistic Prayer 3
page 22 for Eucharistic Prayer 4

EASTER 2

The Lord be with you.	**And also with you.**
Lift up your hearts.	**We lift them up to the Lord.**
Let us give thanks to the Lord our God.	**It is right to give him thanks and praise.**

Father, all-powerful and ever-living God,
we do well always and everywhere to give you thanks
through Jesus Christ our Lord.

We praise you with greater joy than ever in this Easter season,
when Christ became our paschal sacrifice.

In him a new age has dawned,
the long reign of sin is ended,
a broken world has been renewed,
and man is once again made whole.

The joy of the resurrection renews the whole world,
while the choirs of heaven sing for ever to your glory:

Holy, holy, holy Lord, God of power and might,
heaven and earth are full of your glory.
  Hosanna in the highest.

Blessed is he who comes in the name of the Lord.
  Hosanna in the highest.

Turn to
page 15 for Eucharistic Prayer 1
page 18 for Eucharistic Prayer 2
page 20 for Eucharistic Prayer 3
page 22 for Eucharistic Prayer 4

EUCHARISTIC PRAYER 1

(The passages within the brackets may be omitted if the celebrant wishes.)

We come to you, Father,
with praise and thanksgiving,
through Jesus Christ your Son.
Through him we ask you to accept and bless
these gifts we offer you in sacrifice.
We offer them for your holy catholic Church,
watch over it, Lord, and guide it;
grant it peace and unity throughout the world.
We offer them for N. our Pope,
for N. our bishop,
and for all who hold and teach the catholic faith
that comes to us from the apostles.

Remember, Lord, your people,
especially those for whom we now pray, N. and N.
Remember all of us gathered here before you.
You know how firmly we believe in you
and dedicate ourselves to you.
We offer you this sacrifice of praise
for ourselves and those who are dear to us.
We pray to you, our living and true God,
for our well-being and redemption.

In union with the whole Church
we honour Mary,
the ever-virgin mother of Jesus Christ our Lord and God.
We honour Joseph, her husband,
the apostles and martyrs
Peter and Paul, Andrew,
(James, John, Thomas,
James, Philip,
Bartholomew, Matthew, Simon and Jude;
we honour Linus, Cletus, Clement, Sixtus,
Cornelius, Cyprian, Lawrence, Chrysogonus,
John and Paul, Cosmas and Damian)
and all the saints.
May their merits and prayers
gain us your constant help and protection.
(Through Christ our Lord. Amen)

Father, accept this offering
from your whole family.
Grant us your peace in this life,
save us from final damnation,
and count us among those you have chosen.
(Through Christ our Lord. Amen)

Bless and approve our offering;
make it acceptable to you,
an offering in spirit and in truth.
Let it become for us
the body and blood of Jesus Christ,
your only Son, our Lord.

The day before he suffered
he took bread in his sacred hands
and looking up to heaven,
to you, his almighty Father,
he gave you thanks and praise.
He broke the bread,
gave it to his disciples, and said:
Take this, all of you, and eat it:
this is my body which will be given up for you.

When supper was ended, he took the cup.
Again he gave you thanks and praise,
gave the cup to his disciples, and said:
Take this, all of you, and drink from it:
this is the cup of my blood,
the blood of the new and everlasting covenant.
It will be shed for you and for all men
so that sins may be forgiven.
Do this in memory of me.

Let us proclaim the mystery of faith:
1 **Christ has died,**
   Christ is risen,
   Christ will come again.

Alternative acclamations

2 **Dying you destroyed our death,**   3 **When we eat this bread and drink this cup,**
   rising you restored our life.   **we proclaim your death, Lord Jesus,**
   Lord Jesus, come in glory.   **until you come in glory.**

4 **Lord, by your cross and resurrection**
   you have set us free.
   You are the Saviour of the world.

Father, we celebrate the memory of Christ, your Son.
We, your people and your ministers,
recall his passion,
his resurrection from the dead,
and his ascension into glory;
and from the many gifts you have given us
we offer to you, God of glory and majesty,
this holy and perfect sacrifice:
the bread of life
and the cup of eternal salvation.

Look with favour on these offerings
and accept them as once you accepted
the gifts of your servant Abel,
the sacrifice of Abraham, our father in faith,
and the bread and wine offered by your priest Melchisedech.

Almighty God,
we pray that your angel may take this sacrifice
to your altar in heaven.
Then, as we receive from this altar
the sacred body and blood of your Son,
let us be filled with every grace and blessing.
(Through Christ our Lord. Amen.)

Remember, Lord, those who have died
and have gone before us marked with the sign of faith,
especially those for whom we now pray, N. and N.
May these, and all who sleep in Christ,
find in your presence
light, happiness, and peace.
(Through Christ our Lord. Amen.)

For ourselves, too, we ask
some share in the fellowship of your apostles and martyrs,
with John the Baptist, Stephen, Matthias, Barnabas,
(Ignatius, Alexander, Marcellinus, Peter,
Felicity, Perpetua, Agatha, Lucy,
Agnes, Cecilia, Anastasia)
and all the saints.
Though we are sinners,
we trust in your mercy and love.
Do not consider what we truly deserve,
but grant us your forgiveness.

Through Christ our Lord
you give us all these gifts.
You fill them with life and goodness,
you bless them and make them holy.

Through him,
with him,
in him,
in the unity of the Holy Spirit,
all glory and honour is yours,
almighty Father,
for ever and ever.
Amen.

Continue on page 24

EUCHARISTIC PRAYER 2

Lord, you are holy indeed,
the fountain of all holiness.
Let your Spirit come upon these gifts to make them holy,
so that they may become for us
the body and blood of our Lord, Jesus Christ.

Before he was given up to death,
a death he freely accepted,
he took bread and gave you thanks.
He broke the bread,
gave it to his disciples, and said:
Take this, all of you, and eat it:
this is my body which will be given up for you.

When supper was ended, he took the cup.
Again he gave you thanks and praise,
gave the cup to his disciples, and said:
Take this, all of you, and drink from it:
this is the cup of my blood,
the blood of the new and everlasting covenant.
It will be shed for you and for all men
so that sins may be forgiven.
Do this in memory of me.

Let us proclaim the mystery of faith:
1 **Christ has died,
Christ is risen,
Christ will come again.**

Alternative acclamations

2 **Dying you destroyed our death,
rising you restored our life.
Lord Jesus, come in glory.**

3 **When we eat this bread and drink this cup,
we proclaim your death, Lord Jesus,
until you come in glory.**

4 **Lord, by your cross and resurrection
you have set us free.
You are the Saviour of the world.**

In memory of his death and resurrection,
we offer you, Father, this life-giving bread,
this saving cup.
We thank you for counting us worthy
to stand in your presence and serve you.
May all of us who share in the body and blood of Christ
be brought together in unity by the Holy Spirit.

Lord, remember your Church throughout the world;
make us grow in love,
together with N. our Pope,
N. our bishop, and all the clergy.

Remember our brothers and sisters
who have gone to their rest
in the hope of rising again;
bring them and all the departed
into the light of your presence.
Have mercy on us all;
make us worthy to share eternal life
with Mary, the virgin Mother of God,
with the apostles, and with all the saints
who have done your will throughout the ages.
May we praise you in union with them,
and give you glory
through your Son, Jesus Christ.

Through him,
with him,
in him,
in the unity of the Holy Spirit,
all glory and honour is yours,
almighty Father,
for ever and ever.
Amen.

Continue on page 24

EUCHARISTIC PRAYER 3

Father, you are holy indeed,
and all creation rightly gives you praise.
All life, all holiness comes from you
through your Son, Jesus Christ our Lord,
by the working of the Holy Spirit.
From age to age you gather a people to yourself,
so that from east to west
a perfect offering may be made
to the glory of your name.

And so, Father, we bring you these gifts.
We ask you to make them holy by the power of your Spirit,
that they may become the body and blood
of your Son, our Lord Jesus Christ,
by whose command we celebrate this eucharist.

On the night he was betrayed,
he took bread and gave you thanks and praise.
He broke the bread, gave it to his disciples, and said:
Take this, all of you, and eat it:
this is my body which will be given up for you.

When supper was ended, he took the cup.
Again he gave you thanks and praise,
gave the cup to his disciples, and said:
Take this, all of you, and drink from it:
this is the cup of my blood,
the blood of the new and everlasting covenant.
It will be shed for you and for all men
so that sins may be forgiven.
Do this in memory of me.

Let us proclaim the mystery of faith:
**1 Christ has died,
Christ is risen,
Christ will come again.**

Alternative acclamations

**2 Dying you destroyed our death,
rising you restored our life.
Lord Jesus, come in glory.**

**3 When we eat this bread and drink this cup,
we proclaim your death, Lord Jesus,
until you come in glory.**

**4 Lord, by your cross and resurrection
you have set us free.
You are the Saviour of the world.**

Father, calling to mind the death your Son endured for our salvation,
his glorious resurrection and ascension into heaven,
and ready to greet him when he comes again,
we offer you in thanksgiving this holy and living sacrifice.

Look with favour on your Church's offering,
and see the Victim whose death has reconciled us to yourself.
Grant that we, who are nourished by his body and blood,
may be filled with his Holy Spirit,
and become one body, one spirit in Christ.

May he make us an everlasting gift to you
and enable us to share in the inheritance of your saints,
with Mary, the virgin Mother of God;
with the apostles, the martyrs,
(Saint N.—*the patron saint or saint of the day*) and all your saints,
on whose constant intercession we rely for help.

Lord, may this sacrifice,
which has made our peace with you,
advance the peace and salvation of all the world.
Strengthen in faith and love your pilgrim Church on earth;
your servant, Pope N., our bishop N.,
and all the bishops,
with the clergy and the entire people your Son has gained for you.
Father, hear the prayers of the family you have gathered here before you.
In mercy and love unite all your children
wherever they may be.

Welcome into your kingdom our departed brothers and sisters,
and all who have left this world in your friendship.
We hope to enjoy for ever the vision of your glory,
through Christ our Lord, from whom all good things come.

Through him,
with him,
in him,
in the unity of the Holy Spirit,
all glory and honour is yours,
almighty Father,
for ever and ever.
Amen.

Continue on page 24

EUCHARISTIC PRAYER 4

When this Eucharistic Prayer is used the following Preface is always said.

The Lord be with you,	**And also with you.**
Lift up your hearts.	**We lift them up to the Lord.**
Let us give thanks to the Lord our God.	**It is right to give him thanks and praise.**

Father in heaven,
it is right that we should give you thanks and glory:
you alone are God, living and true.

Through all eternity you live in unapproachable light.
Source of life and goodness, you have created all things,
to fill your creatures with every blessing
and lead all men to the joyful vision of your light.

Countless hosts of angels stand before you to do your will;
they look upon your splendour
and praise you, night and day.

United with them,
and in the name of every creature under heaven,
we too praise your glory as we sing [say]:

Holy, holy, holy Lord, God of power and might,
heaven and earth are full of your glory.
    Hosanna in the highest.

Blessed is he who comes in the name of the Lord.
    Hosanna in the highest.

Father, we acknowledge your greatness:
all your actions show your wisdom and love.
You formed man in your own likeness
and set him over the whole world
to serve you, his creator,
and to rule over all creatures.
Even when he disobeyed you and lost your friendship
you did not abandon him to the power of death,
but helped all men to seek and find you.
Again and again you offered a covenant to man,
and through the prophets taught him to hope for salvation.
Father, you so loved the world
that in the fullness of time you sent your only Son to be our Saviour.
He was conceived through the power of the Holy Spirit,
and born of the Virgin Mary,
a man like us in all things but sin.
To the poor he proclaimed the good news of salvation,
to prisoners, freedom,
and to those in sorrow, joy.
In fulfilment of your will
he gave himself up to death;
but by rising from the dead,

he destroyed death and restored life.
And that we might live no longer for ourselves but for him,
he sent the Holy Spirit from you, Father,
as his first gift to those who believe,
to complete his work on earth
and bring us the fullness of grace.

Father, may this Holy Spirit sanctify these offerings.
Let them become the body and blood of Jesus Christ our Lord
as we celebrate the great mystery
which he left us as an everlasting covenant.

He always loved those who were his own in the world.
When the time came for him to be glorified by you, his heavenly Father,
he showed the depth of his love.

While they were at supper,
he took bread, said the blessing, broke the bread
and gave it to his disciples, saying:
Take this, all of you, and eat it:
this is my body which will be given up for you.

In the same way, he took the cup, filled with wine.
He gave you thanks, and giving the cup to his disciples, said:
Take this, all of you, and drink from it:
this is the cup of my blood,
the blood of the new and everlasting covenant.
It will be shed for you and for all men
so that sins may be forgiven.
Do this in memory of me.

Let us proclaim the mystery of faith:

1 **Christ has died,**
  Christ is risen,
  Christ will come again.

2 **Dying you destroyed our death,**
  rising you restored our life.
  Lord Jesus, come in glory.

3 **When we eat this bread and drink this cup,**
  we proclaim your death, Lord Jesus,
  until you come in glory.

4 **Lord, by your cross and resurrection**
  you have set us free.
  You are the Saviour of the world.

Father, we now celebrate this memorial of our redemption.
We recall Christ's death, his descent among the dead,
his resurrection, and his ascension to your right hand;
and, looking forward to his coming in glory,
we offer you his body and blood,
the acceptable sacrifice
which brings salvation to the whole world.

Lord, look upon this sacrifice which you have given to your Church;
and by your Holy Spirit, gather all who share this bread and wine*
into the one body of Christ, a living sacrifice of praise.

Lord, remember those for whom we offer this sacrifice,
especially N. our pope,

(Alternative version in England & Wales)
this one bread and one cup

N. our bishop, and bishops and clergy everywhere.
Remember those who take part in this offering,
those here present and all your people,
and all those who seek you with a sincere heart.
Remember those who have died in the peace of Christ
and all the dead whose faith is known to you alone.
Father, in your mercy grant also to us, your children,
to enter into our heavenly inheritance
in the company of the Virgin Mary, the Mother of God,
and your apostles and saints.
Then, in your kingdom, freed from the corruption of sin and death,
we shall sing your glory with every creature through Christ our Lord,
through whom you give us everything that is good.

Through him,
with him,
in him,
in the unity of the Holy Spirit,
all glory and honour is yours,
almighty Father,
for ever and ever. **Amen.**

COMMUNION RITE

The priest invites everyone to join in the Lord's Prayer in these or similar words:

Let us pray with confidence to the Father
in the words our Saviour gave us:

Our Father, who art in heaven . . .

Deliver us, Lord, from every evil,
and grant us peace in our day.
In your mercy keep us free from sin
and protect us from all anxiety
as we wait in joyful hope
for the coming of our Saviour, Jesus Christ.

**For the kingdom, the power, and the glory are yours,
now and for ever.**

Lord Jesus Christ, you said to your apostles:
I leave you peace, my peace I give you.
Look not on our sins, but on the faith of your Church,
and grant us the peace and unity of your kingdom
where you live for ever and ever.
Amen.

The peace of the Lord be with you always.
And also with you.

Then the priest may add:

Let us offer each other the sign of peace.

All make a sign of peace, according to local custom.

May this mingling of the body and blood of our Lord Jesus Christ bring eternal life to us who receive it.

Lamb of God, you take away the sins of the world:
   have mercy on us.
Lamb of God, you take away the sins of the world:
   have mercy on us.
Lamb of God, you take away the sins of the world:
   grant us peace.

Lord Jesus Christ, Son of the living God, by the will of the Father and the work of the Holy Spirit your death brought life to the world. By your holy body and blood free me from all my sins and from every evil. Keep me faithful to your teaching, and never let me be parted from you.
or
Lord Jesus Christ, with faith in your love and mercy I eat your body and drink your blood. Let it not bring me condemnation, but health in mind and body.

This is the Lamb of God
who takes away the sins of the world.
Happy are those who are called to his supper.
Lord, I am not worthy to receive you,
but only say the word and I shall be healed.

During the distribution of Communion a hymn may be sung. If there is no hymn
Turn to the Proper of the Day *for the Communion Antiphon.*

As the priest offers the host to each person he says: The body of Christ. *The person receiving Communion replies:* **Amen.**

After the communion of the people, a period of silence may be observed, or a hymn may be sung. Then the priest says the Prayer after Communion for which you should
Turn to the Proper of the Day. *Some brief announcements may follow. Then:*

CONCLUDING RITE
The Lord be with you.
And also with you.

The priest blesses the people in these words. On special occasions he may use a more solemn blessing.

May almighty God bless you,
the Father, and the Son, and the Holy Spirit.
Amen.

The priest dismisses the people with one of the following:

The Mass is ended, go in peace. (Alleluia)
Thanks be to God. (Alleluia)

Go in the peace of Christ. (Alleluia)
Thanks be to God. (Alleluia)

Go in peace to love and serve the Lord. (Alleluia)
Thanks be to God. (Alleluia)

As the priest leaves the altar a hymn may be sung.

1st Sunday of Advent

As the priest goes to the altar everyone joins in this Entrance Antiphon or a hymn.

To you, my God, I lift my soul, I trust in you; let me never come to shame. Do not let my enemies laugh at me. No one who waits for you is ever put to shame.

I have lifted up my heart to you, my God. I trust in you; I shall not be put to shame. Do not let my enemies mock me, for no one who relies on you will be disappointed.

Turn to page 4

OPENING PRAYER

All-powerful God,
increase our strength of will for doing good
that Christ may find an eager welcome at his coming
and call us to his side in the kingdom of heaven,
where he lives and reigns with you and the Holy Spirit,
one God, for ever and ever.

Almighty God, grant us the will to greet our Saviour with our good works when he comes, so that we may be worthy to be on his right hand and possess the kingdom of heaven.

FIRST READING   *Jeremiah 33:14-16*

I will make a virtuous Branch grow for David.

See, the days are coming—it is the Lord who speaks—when I am going to fulfil the promise I made to the House of Israel and the House of Judah: "In those days and at that time, I will make a virtuous Branch grow for David, who shall practise honesty and integrity in the land. In those days Judah shall be saved and Israel shall dwell in confidence. And this is the name the city will be called: The Lord-our-integrity."
This is the word of the Lord. **Thanks be to God.**

RESPONSORIAL PSALM   *Psalm 24*

To you, O Lord, I lift up my soul.

1. Lord, make me know your ways.
Lord, teach me your paths.
Make me walk in your truth, and teach me:
for you are God my saviour.

2. The Lord is good and upright.
He shows the path to those who stray,
he guides the humble in the right path;
he teaches his way to the poor.

3. His ways are faithfulness and love
for those who keep his covenant and will.
The Lord's friendship is for those who revere him;
to them he reveals his covenant.

SECOND READING   *I Thessalonians 3:12-4:2*

May the Lord confirm your hearts in holiness when Christ comes.

May the Lord be generous in increasing your love and make you love one another and the whole human race as much as we love you. And may he so confirm your hearts in holiness that you may be blameless in the sight of our God and Father when our Lord Jesus Christ comes with all his saints.

Finally, brothers, we urge you and appeal to you in the Lord Jesus to make more and more progress in the kind of life that you are meant to live: the life that God wants, as you learnt from us, and as you are already living it. You have not forgotten the instructions we gave you on the authority of the Lord Jesus.
This is the word of the Lord. **Thanks be to God.**

All stand to greet the Gospel. If this Acclamation is not sung it may be omitted.
Alleluia, alleluia! Let us see, O Lord, your mercy and give us your saving help. Alleluia!

THE GOSPEL   *Luke 21: 25-28; 34-36*
The Lord be with you. **And also with you.**
A reading from the holy Gospel according to Luke. **Glory to you, Lord.**
Your liberation is near at hand.

Jesus said to his disciples: "There will be signs in the sun and moon and stars; on earth nations in agony, bewildered by the clamour of the ocean and its waves; men dying of fear as they await what menaces the world, for the powers of heaven will be shaken. And then they will see the Son of Man coming in a cloud with power and great glory. When these things begin to take place, stand erect, hold your heads high, because your liberation is near at hand."

"Watch yourselves, or your hearts will be coarsened with debauchery and drunkenness and the cares of life, and that day will be sprung on you suddenly, like a trap. For it will come down on every living man on the face of the earth. Stay awake, praying at all times for the strength to survive all that is going to happen, and to stand with confidence before the Son of Man."
This is the Gospel of the Lord. **Praise to you, Lord Jesus Christ.**

The Homily may follow, then Turn to page 6 for the Creed.

PRAYER OVER THE GIFTS

Father,
from all you give us
we present this bread and wine.
As we serve you now,
accept our offering
and sustain us with your promise of
   eternal life.

Accept, Lord, the gifts we offer, which we have first received from you. You have given us the Mass as a means of grace in this life: may it bring us the reward of eternal salvation.

Turn to page 8 for Advent Preface 1

COMMUNION ANTIPHON
The Lord will shower his gifts, and our land will yield its fruit.

The Lord will show us his goodness, and our earth will yield its fruit.

PRAYER AFTER COMMUNION

Father,
may our communion
teach us to love heaven.
May its promise and hope
guide our way on earth.

You have given us, Lord, your sacrament to help us in this changing world to love the things of heaven and hold fast to what endures for ever. We have received it today: grant that it may be a source of grace for us.

Turn to page 25 for the Concluding Rite.

2nd Sunday of Advent

As the priest goes to the altar everyone joins in this Entrance Antiphon or a hymn.

People of Zion, the Lord will come to save all nations, and your hearts will exult to hear his majestic voice.

Behold, people of Sion, the Lord will come to save the nations.
The Lord in his glory will make his voice heard
and fill your hearts with joy.

Turn to page 4

OPENING PRAYER

God of power and mercy,
open our hearts in welcome.
Remove the things that hinder us
  from receiving Christ with joy,
so that we may share his wisdom
and become one with him
when he comes in glory,
for he lives and reigns with you
  and the Holy Spirit,
one God, for ever and ever.

Almighty and merciful God, grant that the anxieties of this life may not impede us as we hasten to meet your Son. Fill us instead with your heavenly wisdom so that we may come to be united with him: who lives and reigns with you.

FIRST READING
Baruch 5:1-9

God means to show your splendour to every nation.

Jerusalem, take off your dress of sorrow and distress, put on the beauty of the glory of God for ever, wrap the cloak of integrity of God around you, put the diadem of the glory of the Eternal on your head: since God means to show your splendour to every nation under heaven, since the name God gives you for ever will be, "Peace through integrity, and honour through devotedness." Arise, Jerusalem, stand on the heights and turn your eyes to the east: see your sons reassembled from west and east at the command of the Holy One, jubilant that God has remembered them. Though they left you on foot, with enemies for an escort, now God brings them back to you like royal princes carried back in glory. For God has decreed the flattening of each high mountain, of the everlasting hills, the filling of the valleys to make the ground level so that Israel can walk in safety under the glory of God. And the forests and every fragrant tree will provide shade for Israel at the command of God; for God will guide Israel in joy by the light of his glory with his mercy and integrity for escort.
This is the word of the Lord. **Thanks be to God.**

RESPONSORIAL PSALM
Psalm 125

What marvels the Lord worked for us! Indeed we were glad.

1. When the Lord delivered Zion from bondage,
it seemed like a dream.
Then was our mouth filled with laughter,
on our lips there were songs.

2. The heathens themselves said:
"What marvels
the Lord worked for them!"
What marvels the Lord worked for us!
Indeed we were glad.

3. Deliver us, O Lord, from our bondage
as streams in dry land.
Those who are sowing in tears
will sing when they reap.

4. They go out, they go out, full of tears,
carrying seed for the sowing:
they come back, they come back, full of
   song,
carrying their sheaves.

SECOND READING
Philippians 1:3-6; 8-11

Be pure and blameless for the day of Christ.
Every time I pray for all of you, I pray with joy, remembering how you have helped
to spread the Good News from the day you first heard it right up to the present. I am
quite certain that the One who began this good work in you will see that it is finished
when the Day of Christ Jesus comes. God knows how much I miss you all, loving
you as Christ Jesus loves you. My prayer is that your love for each other may
increase more and more and never stop improving your knowledge and deepening
your perception so that you can always recognise what is best. This will help you to
become pure and blameless, and prepare you for the Day of Christ, when you will
reach the perfect goodness which Jesus Christ produces in us for the glory and praise
of God.
This is the word of the Lord. **Thanks be to God.**
All stand to greet the Gospel. If this Acclamation is not sung it may be omitted.
**Alleluia, alleluia! Prepare a way for the Lord, make his paths straight. And all
mankind shall see the salvation of God. Alleluia!**

THE GOSPEL
Luke 3:1-6

The Lord be with you. **And also with you.**
A reading from the holy Gospel according to Luke. **Glory to you, Lord.**
All mankind shall see the salvation of God.
In the fifteenth year of Tiberius Caesar's reign, when Pontius Pilate was governor of
Judaea, Herod tetrarch of Galilee, his brother Philip tetrarch of the lands of Ituraea
and Trachonitis, Lysanias tetrarch of Abilene, during the pontificate of Annas and
Caiaphas, the word of God came to John son of Zechariah, in the wilderness. He
went through the whole Jordan district proclaiming a baptism of repentance for the
forgiveness of sins, as it is written in the book of the sayings of the prophet Isaiah:
A voice cries in the wilderness:
Prepare a way for the Lord,
make his paths straight.
Every valley will be filled in,
every mountain and hill be laid low,
winding ways will be straightened
and rough roads made smooth.
And all mankind shall see the salvation of God.
This is the Gospel of the Lord. **Praise to you, Lord Jesus Christ.**
The Homily may follow, then Turn to page 6 for the Creed.

PRAYER OVER THE GIFTS
Lord,
we are nothing without you.
As you sustain us with your mercy,
receive our prayers and offerings.

Turn to page 8 for Advent Preface 1

Be moved to pity, Lord, by the prayers
and offerings which we unworthy sinners make to you; and though of
ourselves we have no claim on your
favour, in your mercy help and strengthen us.

COMMUNION ANTIPHON

Rise up, Jerusalem, stand on the heights, and see the joy that is coming to you from God.

Arise, Jerusalem, and stand upon the hilltops. See the joy that is coming to you from your God.

PRAYER AFTER COMMUNION

Father,
you give us food from heaven.
By our sharing in this mystery,
teach us to judge wisely the things of
earth and to love the things of heaven.

You have nourished us, Lord, with the bread of heaven. May this sacrament teach us to weigh carefully the things of this world and to love the things of heaven.

Turn to page 25 for the Concluding Rite

3rd Sunday of Advent

As the priest goes to the altar everyone joins in this Entrance Antiphon or a hymn.

Rejoice in the Lord always; again I say, rejoice! The Lord is near.

Rejoice in the Lord always, again I say, Rejoice. The Lord is at hand.

Turn to page 4

OPENING PRAYER

Lord God,
may we, your people,
who look forward to the birthday of
   Christ
experience the joy of salvation
and celebrate that feast with love and
   thanksgiving.

O God, you see your people trustfully waiting for the feast of your Son's birth. Help us to experience the happiness of the salvation he brings, and to recall it in our liturgy with eagerness and joy.

FIRST READING   *Zephaniah 3:14-18*

The Lord will dance with shouts of joy for you as on a day of festival.

Shout for joy, daughter of Zion, Israel, shout aloud! Rejoice, exult with all your heart, daughter of Jerusalem! The Lord has repealed your sentence; he has driven your enemies away. The Lord, the king of Israel, is in your midst; you have no more evil to fear. When that day comes, word will come to Jerusalem: Zion, have no fear, do not let your hands fall limp. The Lord your God is in your midst, a victorious warrior. He will exult with joy over you, he will renew you by his love; he will dance with shouts of joy for you as on a day of festival.

This is the word of the Lord. **Thanks be to God.**

RESPONSORIAL PSALM   *Isaiah 12:2-6*

Sing and shout for joy for great in your midst is the Holy One of Israel.

1. Truly, God is my salvation,
I trust, I shall not fear.
For the Lord is my strength, my song,
he became my saviour.
With joy you will draw water
from the wells of salvation.

2. Give thanks to the Lord, give praise
to his name!
Make his mighty deeds known to the
peoples!
Declare the greatness of his name.

3. Sing a psalm to the Lord
for he has done glorious deeds,
make them known to all the earth!
People of Zion, sing and shout for joy
for great in your midst is the Holy One of Israel.

SECOND READING   *Philippians 4:4-7*

The Lord is very near.

I want you to be happy, always happy in the Lord; I repeat, what I want is your happiness. Let your tolerance be evident to everyone: the Lord is very near. There is no need to worry; but if there is anything you need, pray for it, asking God for it with prayer and thanksgiving, and that peace of God, which is so much greater than we can understand, will guard your hearts and your thoughts, in Christ Jesus. This is the word of the Lord. **Thanks be to God.**

All stand to greet the Gospel. If this Acclamation is not sung it may be omitted.
Alleluia, alleluia! The spirit of the Lord has been given to me. He has sent me to bring good news to the poor. Alleluia!

THE GOSPEL   *Luke 3:10-18*

The Lord be with you. **And also with you.**
A reading from the holy Gospel according to Luke. **Glory to you, Lord.**

What must we do?

When all the people asked John, "What must we do, then?" He answered, "If anyone has two tunics he must share with the man who has none, and the one with something to eat must do the same." There were tax collectors too who came for baptism, and these said to him, "Master, what must we do?" He said to them, "Exact no more than your rate." Some soldiers asked him in their turn, "What about us? What must we do?" He said to them, "No intimidation! No extortion! Be content with your pay!"

A feeling of expectancy had grown among the people, who were beginning to think that John might be the Christ, so John declared before them all, "I baptise you with water, but someone is coming, someone who is more powerful than I am, and I am not fit to undo the strap of his sandals; he will baptise you with the Holy Spirit and fire. His winnowing-fan is in his hand to clear his threshing-floor and to gather the wheat into his barn; but the chaff he will burn in a fire that will never go out." As well as this, there were many other things he said to exhort the people and to announce the Good News to them.

This is the Gospel of the Lord. **Praise to you, Lord Jesus Christ.**

The Homily may follow, then Turn to page 6 for the Creed.

PRAYER OVER THE GIFTS

Lord,
may the gift we offer in faith
  and love
be a continual sacrifice in
  your honour
and truly become our eucharist and
  our salvation.

Lord, grant us the grace ever to be devout in offering you the sacrifice of the Mass, so that we may experience within ourselves the power of the salvation you have won for us.

Turn to pages 8 and 9 for Advent Prefaces 1 or 2

COMMUNION ANTIPHON

Say to the anxious: be strong and fear not, our God will come to save us.

Tell the fainthearted: "Be brave and strong.
Look, our God is coming, and he will save us."

PRAYER AFTER COMMUNION

God of mercy,
may this eucharist bring us your divine help,
free us from our sins,
and prepare us for the birthday of our Saviour,
who is Lord for ever and ever.

In your mercy, Lord, grant our prayer that this sacrament may free us from our faults and make us worthy to celebrate the feast that is approaching.

Turn to page 25 for the Concluding Rite

4th Sunday of Advent

As the priest goes to the altar everyone joins in this Entrance Antiphon or a hymn.

Let the clouds rain down the Just One, and the earth bring forth a Saviour.

Sprinkle your dew, you heavens, from above,
and let the clouds rain down the Just one;
let the earth open and give birth to the Saviour.

Turn to page 4

OPENING PRAYER

Lord,
fill our hearts with your love,
and as you revealed to us by an angel the coming of your Son as man,
so lead us through his suffering and death
to the glory of his resurrection,
for he lives and reigns with you and the Holy Spirit,
one God, for ever and ever.

Lord, enlighten our minds with your grace. You revealed to us through the message of an angel the incarnation of Christ your Son; lead us through his passion and cross to the glory of the resurrection.

FIRST READING   *Micah 5:1-4*

Out of you will be born the one who is to rule over Israel.

The Lord says this: You, (Bethlehem) Ephrathah, the least of the clans of Judah, out of you will be born for me the one who is to rule over Israel; his origin goes back to the distant past, to the days of old. The Lord is therefore going to abandon them till the time when she who is to give birth gives birth. Then the remnant of his brothers will come back to the sons of Israel. He will stand and feed his flock with the power of the Lord, with the majesty of the name of his God. They will live secure, for from then on he will extend his power to the ends of the land. He himself will be peace.
This is the word of the Lord. **Thanks be to God.**

RESPONSORIAL PSALM
Psalm 79

God of hosts, bring us back; let your face shine on us and we shall be saved.

1. O shepherd of Israel, hear us,
shine forth from your cherubim throne.
O Lord, rouse up your might,
O Lord, come to our help.

2. God of hosts, turn again, we implore,
look down from heaven and see.
Visit this vine and protect it,
the vine your right hand has planted.

3. May your hand be on the man you have chosen,
the man you have given your strength.
And we shall never forsake you again:
give us life that we may call upon your name.

SECOND READING
Hebrews 10:5-10

Here I am! I am coming to obey your will.

This is what Christ said, on coming into the world:
You who wanted no sacrifice or oblation, prepared a body for me. You took no pleasure in holocausts or sacrifices for sin; then I said, just as I was commanded in the scroll of the book, "God, here I am! I am coming to obey your will."
Notice that he says first: You did not want what the Law lays down as the things to be offered, that is: the sacrifices, the oblations, the holocausts and the sacrifices for sin, and you took no pleasure in them; and then he says: Here I am! I am coming to obey your will. He is abolishing the first sort to replace it with the second. And this will was for us to be made holy by the offering of his body made once and for all by Jesus Christ.
This is the word of the Lord. **Thanks be to God.**

All stand to greet the Gospel. If this Acclamation is not sung it may be omitted.
Alleluia, alleluia! I am the handmaid of the Lord: let what you have said be done to me. Alleluia!

THE GOSPEL
Luke 1:39-44

The Lord be with you. **And also with you.**
A reading from the holy Gospel according to Luke. **Glory to you, Lord.**
Why should I be honoured with a visit from the mother of my Lord?

Mary set out at that time and went as quickly as she could to a town in the hill country of Judah. She went into Zechariah's house and greeted Elizabeth. Now as soon as Elizabeth heard Mary's greeting, the child leapt in her womb and Elizabeth was filled with the Holy Spirit. She gave a loud cry and said, "Of all women you are the most blessed, and blessed is the fruit of your womb. Why should I be honoured with a visit from the mother of my Lord? For the moment your greeting reached my ears, the child in my womb leapt for joy. Yes, blessed is she who believed that the promise made her by the Lord would be fulfilled."
This is the Gospel of the Lord. **Praise to you, Lord Jesus Christ.**

The Homily may follow, then Turn to page 6 for the Creed.

PRAYER OVER THE GIFTS

Lord,
may the power of the Spirit,
which sanctified Mary the mother of
your Son,
make holy the gifts we place upon this
altar.

Lord, your Spirit filled the Blessed
Virgin's womb with his power. Grant
that the same Spirit may sanctify the
offerings we have placed on your altar.

Turn to pages 8 and 9 for Advent Prefaces 1 or 2

COMMUNION ANTIPHON

The Virgin is with child and shall bear a son, and she will call him Emmanuel.

Behold, a virgin will conceive and give birth to a son, and he will be called Emmanuel.

PRAYER AFTER COMMUNION

Lord,
in this sacrament
we receive the promise of salvation;
as Christmas draws near
make us grow in faith and love
to celebrate the coming of Christ our
Saviour,
who is Lord for ever and ever.

Almighty God, we have received the
pledge of eternal salvation. As we draw
closer to the feast of the day that
brought our salvation, grant that we
may grow worthy of celebrating this
mystery of your Son's birth: who lives
and reigns for ever and ever.

Turn to page 25 for the Concluding Rite

CHRISTMAS

Midnight Mass

As the priest goes to the altar everyone joins in this Entrance Antiphon or a hymn.

The Lord said to me: You are my Son; this day have I begotten you.

The Lord said to me: You are my Son, today I have begotten you.

Turn to page 4

OPENING PRAYER

Father,
you make this holy night radiant
with the splendour of Jesus Christ our
light.
We welcome him as Lord, the true light
of the world.
Bring us to eternal joy in the kingdom of
heaven,
where he lives and reigns with you and
the Holy Spirit,
one God, for ever and ever.

O God, you have brightened this holy
night with the splendour of the true
light. We have learnt to recognise the
mystery of your Son's light on earth:
grant that we may share his joy in
heaven: who lives and reigns with you.

FIRST READING   *Isaiah 9:2-7*
A Son is given to us.

The people that walked in darkness has seen a great light; on those who live in a land of deep shadow a light has shone. You have made their gladness greater, you have made their joy increase; they rejoice in your presence as men rejoice at harvest time, as men are happy when they are dividing the spoils. For the yoke that was weighing on him, the bar across his shoulders, the rod of his oppressor, these you break as on the day of Midian. For all the footgear of battle, every cloak rolled in blood, is burnt, and consumed by fire. For there is a child born for us, a son given to us and dominion is laid on his shoulders; and this is the name they give him: Wonder-Counsellor, Mighty-God, Eternal-Father, Prince-of-Peace. Wide is his dominion in a peace that has no end, for the throne of David and for his royal power, which he establishes and makes secure in justice and integrity. From this time onwards and for ever, the jealous love of the Lord of hosts will do this.
This is the word of the Lord. **Thanks be to God.**

RESPONSORIAL PSALM   *Psalm 95*
Today a saviour has been born to us;
he is Christ the Lord.

1. O sing a new song to the Lord,
   sing to the Lord all the earth.
   O sing to the Lord, bless his name.

2. Proclaim his help day by day,
   tell among the nations his glory
   and his wonders among all the peoples.

3. Let the heavens rejoice and earth be
   glad,
   let the sea and all within it thunder
   praise,
   let the land and all it bears rejoice,
   all the trees of the wood shout for joy
   at the presence of the Lord for he comes,
   he comes to rule the earth.

4. With justice he will rule the world,
   he will judge the peoples with his truth.

SECOND READING   *Titus 2:11-14*
God's grace has been revealed to the whole human race.

God's grace has been revealed, and it has made salvation possible for the whole human race and taught us that what we have to do is to give up everything that does not lead to God, and all our worldly ambitions; we must be self-restrained and live good and religious lives here in this present world, while we are waiting in hope for the blessing which will come with the Appearing of the glory of our great God and saviour Christ Jesus. He sacrificed himself for us in order to set us free from all wickedness and to purify a people so that it could be his very own and would have no ambition except to do good.
This is the word of the Lord. **Thanks be to God.**
All stand to greet the Gospel. If this Acclamation is not sung it may be omitted.
Alleluia, alleluia! I bring you news of great joy: today a saviour has been born to us,
Christ the Lord. Alleluia!

THE GOSPEL
Luke 2:1-14

The Lord be with you. **And also with you.**

A reading from the holy Gospel according to Luke. **Glory to you, Lord.**

Today a saviour has been born to you.

Now at this time Caesar Augustus issued a decree for a census of the whole world to be taken. This census—the first—took place while Quirinius was governor of Syria, and everyone went to his own town to be registered. So Joseph set out from the town of Nazareth in Galilee and travelled up to Judaea, to the town of David called Bethlehem, since he was of David's House and line, in order to be registered together with Mary, his betrothed, who was with child. While they were there the time came to her to have her child, and she gave birth to a son, her first-born. She wrapped him in swaddling clothes, and laid him in a manger because there was no room for them at the inn. In the countryside close by there were shepherds who lived in the fields and took it in turns to watch their flocks during the night. The angel of the Lord appeared to them and the glory of the Lord shone round them. They were terrified, but the angel said, "Do not be afraid. Listen, I bring you news of great joy, a joy to be shared by the whole people. Today in the town of David a saviour has been born to you; he is Christ the Lord. And here is a sign for you: you will find a baby wrapped in swaddling clothes and lying in a manger." And suddenly with the angel there was a great throng of the heavenly host, praising God and singing: "Glory to God in the highest heaven, and peace to men who enjoy his favour".

This is the Gospel of the Lord. **Praise to you, Lord Jesus Christ.**

The Homily may follow, then Turn to page 6 for the Creed.

PRAYER OVER THE GIFTS

Lord,
accept our gifts on this joyful feast of our salvation.
By our communion with God made man,
may we become more like him
who joins our lives to yours,
for he is Lord for ever and ever.

Look favourably, Lord, upon the offering we make to you in honour of today's feast. In your Son our nature is united with you: grant that through this Mass we may grow to be like him: who lives and reigns for ever and ever.

Turn to page 9 for the Christmas Preface

COMMUNION ANTIPHON

The Word of God became man; we have seen his glory.

The Word was made flesh, and we have seen his glory.

PRAYER AFTER COMMUNION

God our Father,
we rejoice in the birth of our Saviour.
May we share his life completely
by living as he has taught.

Lord our God, we celebrate with joy the birthday of our Redeemer. Grant that our lives may make us worthy to be with him for ever in heaven: who lives and reigns for ever and ever.

Turn to page 25 for the Concluding Rite

CHRISTMAS

Dawn Mass

As the priest goes to the altar everyone joins in this Entrance Antiphon or a hymn.

A light will shine on us this day, the Lord is born for us: he shall be called Wonderful God, Prince of peace, Father of the world to come; and his kingship will never end.

Today light will shine on us, for the Lord is born to us.
He will be called Wonderful, God, Prince-of-Peace,
Father of the World to Come; and his reign will be without end.

Turn to page 4

OPENING PRAYER

Father,
we are filled with the new light
by the coming of your Word among us.
May the light of faith
shine in our words and actions.

Almighty God, we are bathed in the new light of your Word made man. Grant that this light which shines in our minds through faith, may be reflected in our deeds.

FIRST READING   *Isaiah 62:11-12*

Look, your saviour comes.

This the Lord proclaims to the ends of the earth: Say to the daughter of Zion, "Look, your saviour comes, the prize of his victory with him, his trophies before him". They shall be called "The Holy People", "The Lord's Redeemed". And you shall be called "The-sought-after", "City-not-forsaken".
This is the word of the Lord. **Thanks be to God.**

RESPONSORIAL PSALM   *Psalm 96*

This day new light will shine upon the earth:
the Lord is born for us.

1. The Lord is king, let earth rejoice,
the many coastlands be glad.
The skies proclaim his justice;
all peoples see his glory.

2. Light shines forth for the just
and joy for the upright of heart.
Rejoice, you just, in the Lord:
give glory to his holy name.

SECOND READING   *Titus: 3:4-7*

It was for no reason except his own compassion that he saved us.

When the kindness and love of God our saviour for mankind were revealed, it was not because he was concerned with any righteous actions we might have done ourselves; it was for no reason except his own compassion that he saved us, by means of the cleansing water of rebirth and by renewing us with the Holy Spirit which he has so generously poured over us through Jesus Christ our saviour. He did this so that we should be justified by his grace, to become heirs looking forward to inheriting eternal life.
This is the word of the Lord. **Thanks be to God.**

All stand to greet the Gospel. If this Acclamation is not sung it may be omitted.
Alleluia, alleluia! Glory to God in the highest heaven, and peace to men who enjoy his favour. Alleluia!

THE GOSPEL   *Luke 2:15–2(*

The Lord be with you. **And also with you.**
A reading from the holy Gospel according to Luke. **Glory to you, Lord.**
The shepherds found Mary and Joseph and the baby.

Now when the angels had gone from them into heaven, the shepherds said to one another, "Let us go to Bethlehem and see this thing that has happened which the Lord has made known to us". So they hurried away and found Mary and Joseph, and the baby lying in the manger. When they saw the child they repeated what they had been told about him, and everyone who heard it was astonished at what the shepherds had to say. As for Mary, she treasured all these things and pondered them in her heart. And the shepherds went back glorifying and praising God for all they had heard and seen; it was exactly as they had been told.
This is the Gospel of the Lord. **Praise to you, Lord Jesus Christ.**

The Homily may follow, then ⌜Turn to page 6 for the Creed.⌟

PRAYER OVER THE GIFTS

Father,
may we follow the example of your Son
who became man and lived among us.
May we receive the gift of divine life
through these offerings here on earth.

Help us, Lord, to offer you our gifts with renewed devotion on this feast of your Son's nativity. Born as a man, he was revealed as God: may these earthly gifts bring us a share in his godhead: who lives and reigns for ever and ever.

⌜Turn to page 9 for the Christmas Preface⌟

COMMUNION ANTIPHON

Daughter of Zion, exult; shout aloud, daughter of Jerusalem! Your King is coming, the Holy One, the Saviour of the world.

Rejoice, daughter of Sion; praise the Lord, daughter of Jerusalem.
See, your King will come, the Holy One, the Saviour of the World.

PRAYER AFTER COMMUNION

Lord,
with faith and joy
we celebrate the birthday of your Son.
Increase our understanding and our love
of the riches you have revealed in him,
who is Lord for ever and ever.

We rejoice, Lord, in celebrating your Son's birth. Help us to peneterate into the depths of this mystery with a greater faith and to welcome it with a warmer love.

⌜Turn to page 25 for the Concluding Rite⌟

CHRISTMAS

Daytime Mass

As the priest goes to the altar everyone joins in this Entrance Antiphon or a hymn.

A child is born for us, a son given to us; dominion is laid on his shoulder, and he shall be called Wonderful-Counsellor.

A child is born to us, a Son is given to us;
the sceptre of princely power is upon his shoulder,
and he is proclaimed the Wonderful Counsellor.

⌜Turn to page 4⌟

OPENING PRAYER

Lord God,
we praise you for creating man,
and still more for restoring him in
  Christ.
Your Son shared our weakness:
may we share his glory,
for he lives and reigns with you
  and the Holy Spirit,
one God, for ever and ever.

O God, when you created man, you
endowed him with a wonderful dignity,
and you restored it to him more perfect
than before. Your Son was willing to
share in our manhood: grant us a share
in his godhead: who lives and reigns
with you.

FIRST READING
Isaiah 52:7-10

All the ends of the earth shall see the salvation of our God.

How beautiful on the mountains, are the feet of one who brings good news, who
heralds peace, brings happiness, proclaims salvation, and tells Zion, "Your God is
king!" Listen! Your watchmen raise their voices, they shout for joy together, for
they see the Lord face to face, as he returns to Zion. Break into shouts of joy
together, you ruins of Jerusalem; for the Lord is consoling his people, redeeming
Jerusalem. The Lord bares his holy arm in the sight of all the nations, and all the
ends of the earth shall see the salvation of our God.
This is the word of the Lord. **Thanks be to God.**

RESPONSORIAL PSALM
Psalm 97

All the ends of the earth have seen the salvation of our God.

1. Sing a new song to the Lord
for he has worked wonders.
His right hand and his holy arm
have brought salvation.

2. The Lord has made known his salvation;
has shown his justice to the nations.
He has remembered his truth and love
for the house of Israel.

3. All the ends of the earth have seen
the salvation of our God.
Shout to the Lord all the earth,
ring out your joy.

4. Sing psalms to the Lord with the
harp,
with the sound of music.
With trumpets and the sound of the horn
acclaim the King, the Lord.

SECOND READING
Hebrews 1:1-6

God has spoken to us through his Son.

At various times in the past and in various ways, God spoke to our ancestors
through the prophets; but in our own time, the last days, he has spoken to us
through his Son, the Son that he has appointed to inherit everything and through
whom he made everything there is. He is the radiant light of God's glory and the
perfect copy of his nature, sustaining the universe by his powerful command; and
now that he has destroyed the defilement of sin, he has gone to take his place in
heaven at the right hand of divine Majesty. So he is now as far above the angels as
the title which he has inherited is higher than their own name.
God has never said to any angel: You are my Son, today I have become your father;
or: I will be a father to him and he a son to me. Again, when he brings the First-born
into the world, he says: Let all the angels of God worship him.
This is the word of the Lord. **Thanks be to God.**

All stand to greet the Gospel. If this Acclamation is not sung it may be omitted.
**Alleluia, alleluia! A hallowed day has dawned upon us. Come, you nations, worship the
Lord, for today a great light has shone down upon the earth. Alleluia!**

THE GOSPEL

John 1:1-18

The Lord be with you. **And also with you.**
A reading from the holy Gospel according to John. **Glory to you Lord.**
The Word was made flesh, and lived among us.

In the beginning was the Word: the Word was with God and the Word was God. He was with God in the beginning. Through him all things came to be, not one thing had its being but through him. All that came to be had life in him and that life was the light of men, a light that shines in the dark a light that darkness could not overpower. A man came, sent by God. His name was John. He came as a witness, as a witness to speak for the light, so that every one might believe through him. He was not the light, only a witness to speak for the light. The Word was the true light that enlightens all men; and he was coming into the world. He was in the world that had its being through him, and the world did not know him. He came to his own domain and his own people did not accept him. But to all who did accept him he gave power to become children of God, to all who believe in the name of him who was born not out of human stock or urge of the flesh or will of man but of God himself. The Word was made flesh, he lived among us, and we saw his glory, the glory that is his as the only Son of the Father, full of grace and truth. John appears as his witness. He proclaims: "This is the one of whom I said: He who comes after me ranks before me because he existed before me". Indeed, from his fulness, we have, all of us, received—yes, grace in return for grace, since, though the Law was given through Moses, grace and truth have come through Jesus Christ. No one has ever seen God; it is the only Son, who is nearest to the Father's heart, who has made him known. This is the Gospel of the Lord. **Praise to you, Lord Jesus Christ.**

The Homily may follow, then Turn to page 6 for the Creed.

PRAYER OVER THE GIFTS

Almighty God,
the saving work of Christ
made our peace with you.
May our offering today
renew that peace within us
and give you perfect praise.

You have given us, Lord, the Mass as a means of mercy and reconciliation, and to be our perfect act of worship. Accept then this offering which we make to you as we celebrate your Son's birth: who lives and reigns for ever and ever.

Turn to page 9 for the Christmas Preface

COMMUNION ANTIPHON

All the ends of the earth have seen the saving power of God.

All the peoples of the earth have seen the saving power of our God.

PRAYER AFTER COMMUNION

Father,
the child born today is the Saviour of the world.
He made us your children,
May he welcome us into your Kingdom where he lives and reigns with you for ever and ever.

God of mercy, the Saviour of the world who was born today brings us your divine life. Grant that he may also confer on us the gift of immortality: who lives and reigns for ever and ever.

Turn to page 25 for the Concluding Rite

The Holy Family

As the priest goes to the altar everyone joins in this Entrance Antiphon or a hymn.

The shepherds hastened to Bethlehem, where they found Mary and Joseph, and the baby lying in a manger.

The shepherds came with haste and found Mary and Joseph, with the Child lying in a manger.

| Turn to page 4 |

OPENING PRAYER

Father,
help us to live as the holy family,
united in respect and love.
Bring us to the joy and peace of your
 eternal home.

O God, you have given us the Holy Family to be our example. Help us to make our homes reflect the loving harmony of that family, so that we may enjoy an eternal reward with you in your heavenly home.

FIRST READING
Ecclesiasticus 3:2-6, 12-14

He who fears the Lord respects his parents.

The Lord honours the father in his children, and upholds the rights of a mother over her sons. Whoever respects his father is atoning for his sins, he who honours his mother is like someone amassing a fortune. Whoever respects his father will be happy with children of his own, he shall be heard on the day when he prays. Long life comes to him who honours his father, he who sets his mother at ease is showing obedience to the Lord. My son, support your father in his old age, do not grieve him during his life. Even if his mind should fail, show him sympathy, do not despise him in your health and strength; for kindness to a father shall not be forgotten but will serve as reparation for your sins.
This is the word of the Lord. **Thanks be to God.**

RESPONSORIAL PSALM
Psalm 127

O blessed are those who fear the Lord and walk in his ways!

1. O blessed are those who fear the Lord
and walk in his ways!
By the labour of your hands you shall
 eat.
You will be happy and prosper.

2. Your wife like a fruitful vine
in the heart of your house;
your children like shoots of the olive,
around your table.

3. Indeed thus shall be blessed
the man who fears the Lord.
May the Lord bless you from Zion
all the days of your life!

SECOND READING
Colossians 3:12-21

Family life in the Lord.

You are God's chosen race, his saints; he loves you, and you should be clothed in sincere compassion, in kindness and humility; gentleness and patience. Bear with one another; forgive each other as soon as a quarrel begins. The Lord has forgiven you; now you must do the same. Over all these clothes, to keep them together and complete them, put on love. And may the peace of Christ reign in your hearts, because it is for this that you were called together as parts of one body. Always be thankful.

Let the message of Christ, in all its richness, find a home with you. Teach each other, and advise each other, in all wisdom. With gratitude in your hearts sing psalms and hymns and inspired songs to God: and never say or do anything except in the name of the Lord Jesus, giving thanks to God the Father through him.

Wives, give way to your husbands, as you should in the Lord. Husbands, love your wives and treat them with gentleness. Children, be obedient to your parents always, because that is what will please the Lord. Parents, never drive your children to resentment or you will make them feel frustrated.

This is the word of the Lord. **Thanks be to God.**

All stand to greet the Gospel. If this Acclamation is not sung it may be omitted.
Alleluia, alleluia! May the peace of Christ reign in your hearts; let the message of Christ find a home with you. Alleluia!

THE GOSPEL   *Luke 2:41-52*

The Lord be with you. **And also with you.**

A reading from the holy Gospel according to Luke. **Glory to you, Lord.**

Jesus is found by his parents sitting among the doctors.

Every year the parents of Jesus used to go to Jerusalem for the feast of the Passover. When he was twelve years old, they went up for the feast as usual. When they were on their way home after the feast, the boy Jesus stayed behind in Jerusalem without his parents knowing it. They assumed he was with the caravan, and it was only after a day's journey that they went to look for him among their relations and acquaintances. When they failed to find him they went back to Jerusalem looking for him everywhere.

Three days later, they found him in the Temple, sitting among the doctors, listening to them, and asking them questions; and all those who heard him were astounded at his intelligence and his replies. They were overcome when they saw him, and his mother said to him, "My child, why have you done this to us? See how worried your father and I have been, looking for you." "Why were you looking for me?" he replied. "Did you not know that I must be busy with my Father's affairs?" But they did not understand what he meant.

He then went down with them and came to Nazareth and lived under their authority. His mother stored up all these things in her heart. And Jesus increased in wisdom, in stature, and in favour with God and men.

This is the Gospel of the Lord. **Praise to you, Lord Jesus Christ.**

PRAYER OVER THE GIFTS

Lord,
accept this sacrifice
and through the prayers of Mary, the
  virgin Mother of God,
and of her husband, Joseph,
unite our families in peace and love.

Accept, Lord, the sacrifice we offer you
and grant, through the intercession o
Our Lady and Saint Joseph, that ou
families may be secure in your grace anc
your peace.

Turn to page 9 for the Christmas Preface

COMMUNION ANTIPHON

Our God has appeared on earth, and lived among men.

Our God has appeared on the earth; and has lived among us.

PRAYER AFTER COMMUNION

Eternal Father,
we want to live as Jesus, Mary, and
   Joseph,
in peace with you and one another.
May this communion strengthen us
to face the troubles of life.

Most merciful Father, you have given us the bread of heaven to renew our strength. Help us to imitate the example of the Holy Family, so that, after the tribulations of this life, we may rejoice in their company for ever.

Turn to page 25 for the Concluding Rite

JANUARY 1: OCTAVE OF CHRISTMAS

Mary, Mother of God

As the priest goes to the altar everyone joins in this Entrance Antiphon or a hymn.

A light will shine on us this day, the Lord is born for us: he shall be called Wonderful God, Prince of peace, Father of the world to come; and his kingship will never end.

Today light will shine on us, for the Lord
   is born to us.
He will be called Wonderful, God,
   Prince of Peace, Father of
the World to come;
and his reign will be without end.

Turn to page 4

OPENING PRAYER

God our Father,
May we always profit by the prayers
of the Virgin Mother Mary,
for you bring us life and salvation
through Jesus Christ her Son
who lives and reigns with you and the
   Holy Spirit,
one God, for ever and ever.

O God, you made Mary's virginity fruitful, and so held out to mankind the reward of eternal salvation. Through her you gave us your Son to be the source of our life: grant that we may experience the power of her prayer for us.

FIRST READING

Numbers 6:22-27

They are to call down my name on the sons of Israel, and I will bless them.

The Lord spoke to Moses and said, "Say this to Aaron and his sons: 'This is how you are to bless the sons of Israel. You shall say to them: May the Lord bless you and keep you. May the Lord let his face shine on you and be gracious to you. May the Lord uncover his face to you and bring you peace.'
"This is how they are to call down my name on the sons of Israel, and I will bless them."
This is the word of the Lord. **Thanks be to God.**

RESPONSORIAL PSALM   *Psalm 66*
O God, be gracious and bless us.

1. God, be gracious and bless us
and let your face shed its light upon us.
So will your ways be known upon earth
and all nations learn your saving help.

2. Let the nations be glad and exult
for you rule the world with justice.
With fairness you rule the peoples,
you guide the nations on earth.

3. Let the peoples praise you, O God;
let all the peoples praise you.
May God still give us his blessing
till the ends of the earth revere him.

SECOND READING   *Galatians 4:4-7*
God sent his Son, born of a woman.

When the appointed time came, God sent his Son, born of a woman, born a subject of the Law, to redeem the subjects of the Law and to enable us to be adopted as sons. The proof that you are sons is that God has sent the Spirit of his Son into our hearts: the Spirit that cries, "Abba, Father," and it is this that makes you a son, you are not a slave any more; and if God has made you son, then he has made you heir.
This is the word of the Lord. **Thanks be to God.**

All stand to greet the Gospel. If this Acclamation is not sung it may be omitted.
Alleluia, alleluia! At various times in the past and in various different ways, God spoke to our ancestors through the prophets; but in our own time, the last days, he has spoken to us through his Son. Alleluia!

THE GOSPEL   *Luke 2:16-21*
The Lord be with you. **And also with you.**
A reading from the holy Gospel according to Luke. **Glory to you, Lord.**

They found Mary and Joseph and the babe . . . When the eighth day came, they gave him the name Jesus.

The shepherds hurried away to Bethlehem and found Mary and Joseph, and the baby lying in the manger. When they saw the child they repeated what they had been told about him, and everyone who heard it was astonished at what the shepherds had to say. As for Mary, she treasured all these things and pondered them in her heart. And the shepherds went back glorifying and praising God, for all they had heard and seen; it was exactly as they had been told.
When the eighth day came and the child was to be circumcised they gave him the name Jesus, the name the angel had given him before his conception.
This is the Gospel of the Lord. **Praise to you, Lord Jesus Christ.**

The Homily may follow, then Turn to page 6 for the Creed.

PRAYER OVER THE GIFTS

God our Father,
we celebrate at this season
the beginning of our salvation.
On this feast of Mary, the Mother of God,
we ask that our salvation
will be brought to its fulfilment.

God of love, all that is good owes its existence and its perfection to you. On this feast of the holy Mother of God, we acknowledge gladly the grace you have given us in the past: bring it now, we pray, to joyful fulfilment.

Turn to page 8 for Preface

COMMUNION ANTIPHON

Jesus Christ is the same yesterday, today and for ever.

Jesus Christ is the same yesterday and today; and will be the same for ever and ever.

PRAYER AFTER COMMUNION

Father,
as we proclaim the Virgin Mary
to be the mother of Christ and the
  mother of the Church,
may our communion with her Son
bring us to salvation.

Lord, on this feast we gladly proclaim Mary, ever Virgin, as the mother of your Son and of the Church. With joy we have received the Bread of heaven: grant that it may enable us to attain eternal life.

Turn to page 25 for the Concluding Rite

2nd Sunday after Christmas

As the priest goes to the altar everyone joins in this Entrance Antiphon or a hymn.

When peaceful silence lay over all, and night had run half of her swift course, your all-powerful word, O Lord, leaped down from heaven, from the royal throne.

While the midnight silence reigned over all, and the night was now half-spent, your almighty Word, O God, leapt down from his royal throne in heaven.

Turn to page 4

OPENING PRAYER

God of power and life,
glory of all who believe in you,
fill the world with your splendour
and show the nations the light of your
  truth.

Almighty, eternal God, light of souls that are faithful to you, fill the world with your glory and reveal yourself to all nations in the radiance of your light.

FIRST READING
Sirach 24:1-4, 12-16

The wisdom of God has pitched her tent among the chosen people.

Wisdom speaks her own praises, in the midst of her people she glories in herself. She opens her mouth in the assembly of the Most High, she glories in herself in the presence of the Mighty One; "I came forth from the mouth of the Most High, and I covered the earth like mist. I had my tent in the heights, and my throne in a pillar of cloud. Then the creator of all things instructed me, and he who created me fixed a place for my tent. He said, 'Pitch your tent in Jacob, make Israel your inheritance'. From eternity, in the beginning, he created me, and for eternity I shall remain. I ministered before him in the holy tabernacle, and thus was I established on Zion. In the beloved city he has given me rest, and in Jerusalem I wield my authority. I have taken root in a privileged people, in the Lord's property, in his inheritance." This is the word of the Lord. **Thanks be to God.**

RESPONSORIAL PSALM   *Psalm 147*
The Word was made flesh, and lived among us. Alleluia!

1. O Praise the Lord, Jerusalem!
Zion, praise your God!
He has strengthened the bars
   of your gates,
he has blessed the children within you.

2. He established peace on your borders,
he feeds you with finest wheat.
He sends out his word to the earth
and swiftly runs his command.

3. He makes his word known to Jacob,
to Israel his laws and decrees.
He has not dealt thus with other nations;
he has not taught them his decrees.
Alleluia!

SECOND READING   *Ephesians 1:3-6, 15-18*
He determined that we should become his adopted sons through Jesus.
Blessed be God the Father of our Lord Jesus Christ, who has blessed us with all the spiritual blessings of heaven in Christ. Before the world was made, he chose us, chose us in Christ, to be holy and spotless, and to live through love in his presence, determining that we should become his adopted sons, through Jesus Christ, for his own kind purposes, to make us praise the glory of his grace, his free gift to us in the Beloved.
That will explain why I, having once heard about your faith in the Lord Jesus, and the love that you show towards all the saints, have never failed to remember you in my prayers and to thank God for you. May the God of our Lord Jesus Christ, the Father of glory, give you a spirit of wisdom and perception of what is revealed, to bring you to full knowledge of him. May he enlighten the eyes of your mind so that you can see what hope his call holds for you, what rich glories he has promised the saints will inherit.
This is the word of the Lord. **Thanks be to God.**
All stand to greet the Gospel. If this Acclamation is not sung it may be omitted.
Alleluia, alleluia! Glory be to you, O Christ, proclaimed to the pagans; Glory be to you, O Christ, believed in by the world. Alleluia!

THE GOSPEL   *John 1:1-18*
The Lord be with you. **And also with you.**
A reading from the holy Gospel according to John. **Glory to you, Lord.**
The Word was made flesh, and lived among us.
In the beginning was the Word: the Word was with God and the Word was God. He was with God in the beginning. Through him all things came to be, not one thing had its being but through him. All that came to be had life in him and that life was the light of men, a light that shines in the dark, a light that darkness could not

overpower. A man came, sent by God. His name was John. He came as a witness, as a witness to speak for the light, so that everyone might believe through him. He was not the light, only a witness to speak for the light. The Word was the true light that enlightens all men; and he was coming into the world. He was in the world that had its being through him, and the world did not know him. He came to his own domain and his own people did not accept him. But to all who did accept him he gave power to become children of God, to all who believe in the name of him who was born not out of human stock or urge of the flesh or will of man but of God himself. The Word was made flesh, he lived among us, and we saw his glory, the glory that is his as the only Son of the Father, full of grace and truth. John appears as his witness. He proclaims: "This is the one of whom I said: He who comes after me ranks before me because he existed before me". Indeed, from his fulness we have, all of us, received—yes, grace in return for grace, since though the Law was given through Moses, grace and truth have come through Jesus Christ. No one has ever seen God; it is the only Son, who is nearest to the Father's heart, who has made him known. This is the Gospel of the Lord. **Praise to you, Lord Jesus Christ.**

The Homily may follow, then *Turn to page 6 for the Creed.*

PRAYER OVER THE GIFTS

Lord,
make holy these gifts
through the coming of your Son,
who shows us the way of truth
and promises the life of your kingdom.

Sanctify, Lord, the gifts we offer you as we celebrate your Son's birth; it reveals to us the true way of life in this world and brings us the promise of eternal life in heaven.

Turn to page 9 for the Christmas Preface

COMMUNION ANTIPHON

He gave to all who accepted him the power to become children of God.

To all who welcomed him, He gave the right to become sons of God.

PRAYER AFTER COMMUNION

Lord,
hear our prayers.
By this eucharist free us from sin
and keep us faithful in your word.

Lord God, we pray, by the power of this sacrament cleanse us from our faults and fulfil our holy desires.

Turn to page 25 for the Concluding Rite

JANUARY 6

Epiphany

As the priest goes to the altar everyone joins in this Entrance Antiphon or a hymn.

The Lord and ruler is coming; kingship is his, and government and power.

Behold, God the Mighty has come; power, rule and dominion are in his hands.

Turn to page 4

OPENING PRAYER

Father,
you revealed your Son to the nations
by the guidance of a star.
Lead us to your glory in heaven
by the light of faith.

O God, on this day you led the gentiles
by a star and revealed to them your Son.
We know you now by faith: lead us on
to the sight of your heavenly glory.

FIRST READING
Isaiah 60:1-6

Above you the glory of the Lord appears.

Arise, shine out, for your light has come, the glory of the Lord is rising on you, though night still covers the earth and darkness the peoples. Above you the Lord now rises and above you his glory appears. The nations come to your light and kings to your dawning brightness. Lift up your eyes and look round: all are assembling and coming towards you, your sons from far away and your daughters being tenderly carried. At this sight you will grow radiant, your heart throbbing and full; since the riches of the sea will flow to you, the wealth of the nations come to you; camels in throngs will cover you, and dromedaries of Midian and Ephah; everyone in Sheba will come, bringing gold and incense and singing the praise of the Lord. This is the word of the Lord. **Thanks be to God.**

RESPONSORIAL PSALM
Psalm 71

All nations shall fall prostrate before you, O Lord.

1. O God, give your judgement to the king,
to a king's son your justice,
that he may judge your people in justice
and your poor in right judgement.

2. In his days justice shall flourish
and peace till the moon fails.
He shall rule from sea to sea,
from the Great River to earth's bounds.

3. The kings of Tarshish and the sea coasts
shall pay him tribute.
The kings of Sheba and Seba
shall bring him gifts.
Before him all kings shall fall prostrate,
all nations shall serve him.

4. For he shall save the poor when they cry
and the needy who are helpless.
He will have pity on the weak
and save the lives of the poor.

SECOND READING
Ephesians 3:2-3a, 5-6

This mystery has now been revealed: it means that pagans now share the same inheritance.

You have probably heard how I have been entrusted by God with the grace he meant for you, and that it was by a revelation that I was given the knowledge of the mystery.
This mystery that has now been revealed through the Spirit to his holy apostles and prophets was unknown to any men in past generations; it means that pagans now share the same inheritance, that they are parts of the same body, and that the same promise has been made to them, in Christ Jesus, through the gospel. This is the word of the Lord. **Thanks be to God.**

All stand to greet the Gospel. If this Acclamation is not sung it may be omitted.
Alleluia, alleluia! We saw his star as it rose and have come to do the Lord homage. Alleluia!

THE GOSPEL *Matthew 2:1-12*

The Lord be with you. **And also with you.**

A reading from the holy Gospel according to Matthew. **Glory to you, Lord.**

We came from the east to do the king homage.

After Jesus had been born at Bethlehem in Judaea during the reign of King Herod, some wise men came to Jerusalem from the east. "Where is the infant king of the Jews!" they asked. "We saw his star as it rose and have come to do him homage." When King Herod heard this he was perturbed, and so was the whole of Jerusalem. He called together all the chief priests and the scribes of the people, and enquired of them where the Christ was to be born. "At Bethlehem in Judaea," they told him "for this is what the prophet wrote: And you, Bethlehem, in the land of Judah, you are by no means least among the leaders of Judah, for out of you will come a leader who will shepherd my people Israel." Then Herod summoned the wise men to see him privately. He asked them the exact date on which the star had appeared, and sent them on to Bethlehem. "Go and find out all about the child," he said "and when you have found him, let me know, so that I too may go and do him homage." Having listened to what the king had to say, they set out. And there in front of them was the star they had seen rising; it went forward and halted over the place where the child was. The sight of the star filled them with delight, and going into the house they saw the child with his mother Mary, and falling to their knees they did him homage. Then, opening their treasures, they offered him gifts of gold and frankincense and myrrh. But they were warned in a dream not to go back to Herod, and returned to their own country by a different way.

This is the Gospel of the Lord. **Praise to you, Lord Jesus Christ.**

The Homily may follow, then | *Turn to page 6 for the Creed.* |

PRAYER OVER THE GIFTS

Lord,
accept the offerings of your Church,
not gold, frankincense and myrrh,
but the sacrifice and food they symbolise:
Jesus Christ, who is Lord for ever and ever.

Look favourably, Lord, upon your Church's gifts. We do not offer gold, incense and myrrh; we offer Jesus Christ, for through our gifts of bread and wine he is signified, sacrificed and received.

| *Turn to page 10 for the Preface of the Epiphany* |

COMMUNION ANTIPHON

We have seen his star in the east, and have come with gifts to adore the Lord.

We have seen his star rising in the east, and we have come with our gifts to pay him homage.

PRAYER AFTER COMMUNION

Father,
guide us with your light.
Help us to recognise Christ in this eucharist
and welcome him with love,
for he is Lord for ever and ever.

Lord, give us always your heavenly light to lead us at every step we take. Strengthen our faith in this sacrament so that we may always receive it with due devotion.

| *Turn to page 25 for the Concluding Rite* |

SUNDAY AFTER JANUARY 6

The Baptism of the Lord

As the priest goes to the altar everyone joins in this Entrance Antiphon or a hymn.

When the Lord had been baptized the heavens opened, and the Spirit came down like a dove to rest on him. Then the voice of the Father thundered: This is my beloved Son, with him I am well pleased.

When Christ was baptized the heavens opened;
the Holy Spirit appeared as a dove resting on him;
the voice of the Father proclaimed:
This is my beloved Son, with whom I am well pleased.

Turn to page 4

OPENING PRAYER

Almighty, eternal God,
when the Spirit descended upon Jesus
at his baptism in the Jordan,
you revealed him as your own beloved
 Son.
Keep us, your children born of water
 and the Spirit,
faithful to our calling.

Almighty, eternal God, when Christ had been baptized in the Jordan, the Holy Spirit came down on him and you solemnly proclaimed him to be your beloved Son. We are your sons and daughters by adoption, born again by water and the Holy Spirit. Grant that with us you may always be well pleased.

FIRST READING   *Isaiah 42:1-4, 6-7*

Here is my servant in whom my soul delights.

Thus says the Lord: Here is my servant whom I uphold, my chosen one in whom my soul delights. I have endowed him with my spirit that he may bring true justice to the nations. He does not cry out or shout aloud, or make his voice heard in the streets. He does not break the crushed reed, nor quench the wavering flame. Faithfully he brings true justice; he will neither waver, nor be crushed until true justice is established on earth, for the islands are awaiting his law. I, the Lord, have called you to serve the cause of right; I have taken you by the hand and formed you; I have appointed you as covenant of the people and light of nations, to open the eyes of the blind, to free captives from prison, and those who live in darkness from the dungeon.
This is the word of the Lord. **Thanks be to God.**

RESPONSORIAL PSALM   *Psalm 28*

The Lord will bless his people with peace.

1. O give the Lord you sons of God,
give the Lord glory and power;
give the Lord the glory of his name.
Adore the Lord in his holy court.

2. The Lord's voice resounding on the waters,
the Lord on the immensity of waters;
the voice of the Lord, full of power,
the voice of the Lord, full of splendour.

3. The God of glory thunders.
In his temple they all cry: "Glory!"
The Lord sat enthroned over the flood;
the Lord sits as king for ever.

SECOND READING   *Acts 10:34-38*

The Lord has anointed him with the Holy Spirit.

Peter addressed Cornelius and his household: "The truth I have now come to
realise," he said, "is that God does not have favourites, but that anybody of any
nationality who fears God and does what is right is acceptable to him.
"It is true, God sent his word to the people of Israel, and it was to them that the good
news of peace was brought by Jesus Christ—but Jesus Christ is Lord of all men. You
must have heard about the recent happenings in Judaea; about Jesus of Nazareth
and how he began in Galilee, after John had been preaching baptism. God had
anointed him with the Holy Spirit and with power, and because God was with him,
Jesus went about doing good and curing all who had fallen into the power of the
devil."

This is the word of the Lord. **Thanks be to God.**

All stand to greet the Gospel. If this Acclamation is not sung it may be omitted.

**Alleluia, alleluia! The heavens opened and the Father's voice resounded: "This is my
Son, the Beloved. Listen to him." Alleluia!**

THE GOSPEL   *Luke 3:15-16, 21-22*

The Lord be with you. **And also with you.**

A reading from the holy Gospel according to Luke. **Glory to you, Lord.**

While Jesus after his own baptism was at prayer, heaven opened.

A feeling of expectancy had grown among the people, who were beginning to think
that John might be the Christ, so John declared before them all, "I baptise you with
water, but someone is coming, someone who is more powerful than I am, and I am
not fit to undo the strap of his sandals; he will baptise you with the Holy Spirit and
fire."

Now when all the people had been baptised and while Jesus after his own baptism
was at prayer, heaven opened and the Holy Spirit descended on him in bodily shape,
like a dove. And a voice came from heaven, "You are my Son, the Beloved; my
favour rests on you."

This is the Gospel of the Lord. **Praise to you, Lord Jesus Christ.**

The Homily may follow, then | Turn to page 6 for the Creed. |

PRAYER OVER THE GIFTS

Lord,
we celebrate the revelation of Christ
  your Son
who takes away the sins of the world.
Accept our gifts
and let them become one with his
  sacrifice,
for he is Lord for ever and ever.

Accept, Lord, the gifts we offer you as
we celebrate the revealing of your beloved Son. In his mercy he chose to atone
for the sins of the world; grant that your
people's offering of bread and wine may
become his sacrifice: who lives and
reigns for ever and ever.

| Turn to page 8 for the Preface |

COMMUNION ANTIPHON

**This is he of whom John said: I have seen
and have given witness that this is the Son
of God.**

**This is the One of whom the Baptist said:
I have seen him myself and I can bear
      testimony
that he is the Son of God.**

PRAYER AFTER COMMUNION

Lord,
you feed us with bread from heaven.
May we hear your Son with faith
and become your children in name and
in fact.

You have nourished us, Lord, with your
sacred gift; grant that we may listen to
your Son in faith, and may ourselves not
only be called your sons but truly be so.

Turn to page 25 for the Concluding Rite

2nd Sunday of the Year

As the priest goes to the altar everyone joins in this Entrance Antiphon or a hymn.

May all the earth give you worship and praise, and break into song to your name, O God, Most High.

Let all the world adore you, God most High, and hymn your praises; may all proclaim your power and might.

Turn to page 4

OPENING PRAYER

Father of heaven and earth,
hear our prayers,
and show us the way to peace in the
world.

Almighty, eternal God, ruler of all
things both in heaven and on earth,
listen favourably to the petitions of your
people, and grant us peace in our time.

FIRST READING *Isaiah 62:1-5*

The bridegroom rejoices in his bride.

About Zion I will not be silent, about Jerusalem I will not grow weary, until her
integrity shines out like the dawn and her salvation flames like a torch.
The nations then will see your integrity, all the kings your glory, and you will be
called by a new name, one which the mouth of the Lord will confer. You are to be a
crown of splendour in the hand of the Lord, a princely diadem in the hand of your
God; no longer are you to be named "Forsaken", nor your land "Abandoned", but
you shall be called "My Delight" and your land "The Wedded"; for the Lord takes
delight in you and your land will have its wedding. Like a young man marrying a
virgin, so will the one who built you wed you, and as the bridegroom rejoices in his
bride, so will your God rejoice in you.
This is the word of the Lord. **Thanks be to God.**

RESPONSORIAL PSALM *Psalm 95*

Proclaim the wonders of the Lord among all the peoples.

1. O sing a new song to the Lord,
sing to the Lord all the earth.
O sing to the Lord, bless his name.

2. Proclaim his help day by day,
tell among the nations his glory
and his wonders among all the peoples.

3. Give the Lord, you families of
peoples,
give the Lord glory and power,
give the Lord the glory of his name.

4. Worship the Lord in his temple.
O earth, tremble before him.
Proclaim to the nations: "God is king."
He will judge the peoples in fairness.

SECOND READING *I Corinthians 12:4-11*

One and the same Spirit, who distributes gifts to different people just as he chooses.

There is a variety of gifts but always the same Spirit; there are all sorts of service to be done, but always to the same Lord; working in all sorts of different ways in different people, it is the same God who is working in all of them. The particular way in which the Spirit is given to each person is for a good purpose. One may have the gift of preaching with wisdom given him by the Spirit; another may have the gift of preaching instruction given him by the same Spirit; and another the gift of faith given by the same Spirit; another again the gift of healing, through this one Spirit; one, the power of miracles; another, prophecy; another the gift of recognising spirits; another the gift of tongues and another the ability to interpret them. All these are the work of one and the same Spirit, who distributes different gifts to different people just as he chooses.

This is the word of the Lord. **Thanks be to God.**

All stand to greet the Gospel. If this Acclamation is not sung it may be omitted.
Alleluia, alleluia! Your words are spirit, Lord, and they are life: you have the message of eternal life. Alleluia!

THE GOSPEL   *John 2:1-12*

The Lord be with you. **And also with you.**
A reading from the holy Gospel according to John. **Glory to you, Lord.**

This was the first of the signs given by Jesus: it was given at Cana in Galilee.

There was a wedding at Cana in Galilee. The mother of Jesus was there, and Jesus and his disciples had also been invited. When they ran out of wine, since the wine provided for the wedding was all finished, the mother of Jesus said to him, "They have no wine." Jesus said, "Woman, why turn to me? My hour has not yet come." His mother said to the servants, "Do whatever he tells you." There were six stone water jars standing there, meant for the ablutions that are customary among the Jews: each could hold twenty or thirty gallons. Jesus said to the servants, "Fill the jars with water," and they filled them to the brim. "Draw some out now" he told them "and take it to the steward." They did this; the steward tasted the water, and it had turned into wine. Having no idea where it came from—only the servants who had drawn the water knew—the steward called the bridegroom and said, "People generally serve the best wine first, and keep the cheaper sort till the guests have had plenty to drink; but you have kept the best wine till now."

This was the first of the signs given by Jesus: it was given at Cana in Galilee. He let his glory be seen, and his disciples believed in him. After this he went down to Capernaum with his mother and the brothers, but they stayed there only a few days.

This is the Gospel of the Lord. **Praise to you, Lord Jesus Christ.**

The Homily may follow, then *Turn to page 6 for the Creed.*

PRAYER OVER THE GIFTS

Father,
may we celebrate the eucharist
with reverence and love,
for when we proclaim the death of the
     Lord
you continue the work of his redemp-
     tion,
who is Lord for ever and ever.

Grant us the grace, we pray you Lord, to take part worthily in this Mass; for whenever the memorial of Christ, our sacrifice, is celebrated, the work of our redemption is accomplished.

Turn to pages 10 and 11 for the Sunday Prefaces

54

COMMUNION ANTIPHON

The Lord has prepared a feast for me: given wine in plenty for me to drink.

You have prepared a table for me, your Precious Blood you have given me; how wonderful it is!

PRAYER AFTER COMMUNION

Lord,
you have nourished us with bread
  from heaven.
Fill us with your Spirit,
and make us one in peace and love.

Fill us, Lord, with the Spirit of your love. You have given us the one bread of heaven to eat: unite us in loving care for one another.

Turn to page 25 for the Concluding Rite

3rd Sunday of the Year

As the priest goes to the altar everyone joins in this Entrance Antiphon or a hymn.

Sing a new song to the Lord! Sing to the Lord, all the earth. Truth and beauty surround him, he lives in holiness and glory.

Sing to the Lord a new song; all the world sing to the Lord.
Majesty and glory attend him;
holiness and power are in his sanctuary.

Turn to page 4

OPENING PRAYER

All-powerful and ever-living God,
direct your love that is within us,
that our efforts in the name of your Son
may bring mankind to unity and peace.

Almighty, eternal God, guide our actions according to your will, so that we may be fruitful in good works through the grace of your beloved Son.

FIRST READING   *Nehemiah 8:2-6, 8-10*

Ezra read from the law of God and the people understood what was read.

Ezra the priest brought the Law before the assembly, consisting of men, women, and children old enough to understand. This was the first day of the seventh month. On the square before the Water Gate, in the presence of the men and women, and children old enough to understand, he read from the book from early morning till noon; all the people listened attentively to the Book of the Law.

Ezra the scribe stood on a wooden dais erected for the purpose. In full view of all the people—since he stood higher than all the people—Ezra opened the book; and when he opened it all the people stood up. Then Ezra blessed the Lord, the great God, and all the people raised their hands and answered, "Amen! Amen!"; then they bowed down and, face to the ground, prostrated themselves before the Lord. And Ezra read from the Law of God, translating and giving the sense, so that the people understood what was read.

Then (Nehemiah—His Excellency—and) Ezra, priest and scribe (and the Levites who were instructing the people) said to all the people, "This day is sacred to the Lord your God. Do not be mournful, do not weep." For the people were all in tears as they listened to the words of the Law.

He then said, "Go, eat the fat, drink the sweet wine, and send a portion to the man

who has nothing prepared ready. For this day is sacred to our Lord. Do not be sad: the joy of the Lord is your stronghold."
This is the word of the Lord. **Thanks be to God.**

RESPONSORIAL PSALM   *Psalm 18*
Your words are spirit, Lord, and they are life.

1. The law of the Lord is perfect,
it revives the soul.
The rule of the Lord is to be trusted,
it gives wisdom to the simple.

2. The precepts of the Lord are right,
they gladden the heart.
The command of the Lord is clear,
it gives light to the eyes.

3. The fear of the Lord is holy,
abiding for ever.
The decrees of the Lord are truth
my rescuer, my rock!

4. May the spoken words of my mouth,
the thoughts of my heart,
win favour in your sight, O Lord,
my rescuer, my rock!

SECOND READING   *I Corinthians 12:12-30*
You together are Christ's body; but each of you is a different part of it.

Just as a human body, though it is made up of many parts, is a single unit because all these parts, though many, make one body, so it is with Christ. In the one Spirit we were all baptised, Jews as well as Greeks, slaves as well as citizens, and one Spirit was given to us all to drink.

Nor is the body to be identified with any one of its many parts. If the foot were to say, "I am not a hand and so I do not belong to the body", would that mean that it stopped being part of the body? If the ear were to say, "I am not an eye, and so I do not belong to the body," would that mean that it was not a part of the body? If your whole body was just one eye, how would you hear anything? If it was just one ear, how would you smell anything?

Instead of that, God put all the separate parts into the body on purpose. If all the parts were the same, how could it be a body? As it is, the parts are many but the body is one. The eye cannot say to the hand, "I do not need you," nor can the head say to the feet, "I do not need you."

What is more, it is precisely the the parts of the body that seem to be the weakest which are the indispensable ones; and it is the least honourable parts of the body that we clothe with the greatest care. So our more improper parts get decorated in a way that our more proper parts do not need. God has arranged the body so that more dignity is given to the parts which are without it, and so that there may not be disagreements inside the body, but that each part may be equally concerned for all the others. If one part is hurt, all parts are hurt with it. If one part is given special honour, all parts enjoy it.

Now you together are Christ's body; but each of you is a different part of it. In the Church, God has given the first place to apostles, the second to prophets, the third to teachers; after them, miracles, and after them the gift of healing; helpers, good leaders, those with many languages. Are all of them apostles, or all of them prophets, or all of them teachers? Do they all have the gift of miracles, or all have the gift of healing? Do all speak strange languages, and all interpret them?
This is the word of the Lord. **Thanks be to God.**

All stand to greet the Gospel. If this Acclamation is not sung it may be omitted.
Alleluia, alleluia! The Lord has sent me to bring the Good News to the poor, to proclaim liberty to the captives. Alleluia!

THE GOSPEL   *Luke 1:1-4; 4:14-21*
The Lord be with you. **And also with you.**
A reading from the holy Gospel according to Luke. **Glory to you, Lord.**
This text is being fulfilled today.
Seeing that many others have undertaken to draw up accounts of the events that
have taken place among us, exactly as these were handed down to us by those who
from the outset were eyewitnesses and ministers of the word, I in my turn, after
carefully going over the whole story from the beginning, have decided to write an
ordered account for you, Theophilus, so that your Excellency may learn how well
founded the teaching is that you have received.
Jesus, with the power of the Spirit in him, returned to Galilee; and his reputation
spread throughout the countryside. He taught in their synagogues and everyone
praised him.
He came to Nazara, where he had been brought up, and went into the synagogue on
the sabbath day as he usually did. He stood up to read, and they handed him the
scroll of the prophet Isaiah. Unrolling the scroll he found the place where it is
written: The Spirit of the Lord has been given to me, for he has anointed me. He has
sent me to bring the good news to the poor, to proclaim liberty to captives and to the
blind new sight, to set the downtrodden free, to proclaim the Lord's year of favour.
He then rolled up the scroll, gave it back to the assistant and sat down. And all eyes
in the synagogue were fixed on him. Then he began to speak to them, "This text is
being fulfilled today even as you listen."
This is the Gospel of the Lord. **Praise to you, Lord Jesus Christ.**

The Homily may follow, then *Turn to page 6 for the Creed.*

PRAYER OVER THE GIFTS
Lord,   Lord, be appeased and receive our gifts:
receive our gifts.   sanctify them, so that they may bring us
Let our offerings make us holy   salvation.
and bring us salvation.

Turn to pages 10 and 11 for the Sunday Prefaces

COMMUNION ANTIPHON
Look up at the Lord with gladness and   **Come to the Lord and receive his light;**
smile; your face will never be ashamed.   **turn away in shame no longer.**

PRAYER AFTER COMMUNION
God, all-powerful Father,   Grant us, we pray, almighty God, that
may the new life you give us   your grace may be a source of life to us,
   increase our love   and this gift we have received, a source
and keep us in the joy of your kingdom.   of joy.

Turn to page 25 for the Concluding Rite

4th Sunday of the Year

As the priest goes to the altar everyone joins in this Entrance Antiphon or a hymn.

Save us, Lord our God, and gather us together from the nations, that we may proclaim your holy name and glory in your praise.

Lord our God, save us; gather us together from all parts of the earth; let us give thanks to you and find glory in your praise.

Turn to page 4

OPENING PRAYER

Lord our God, help us to love you with all our hearts and to love all men as you love them.

Grant us, Lord our God, that we may worship you with all devotion, and seek to love all men according to your will.

FIRST READING
Jeremiah 1:4-5, 17-19

I have appointed you as prophet to the nations.

The word of the Lord was addressed to me, saying, "Before I formed you in the womb I knew you; before you came to birth I consecrated you; I have appointed you as prophet to the nations. So now brace yourself for action. Stand up and tell them all I command you. Do not be dismayed at their presence, or in their presence I will make you dismayed. I, for my part, today will make you into a fortified city, a pillar of iron, and a wall of bronze to confront all this land: the kings of Judah, its princes, its priests and the country people. They will fight against you but shall not overcome you, for I am with you to deliver you— it is the Lord who speaks." This is the word of the Lord. **Thanks be to God.**

RESPONSORIAL PSALM
Psalm 70

My lips will tell of your help.

1. In you, O Lord, I take refuge;
let me never be put to shame.
In your justice rescue me, free me:
pay heed to me and save me.

2. Be a rock where I can take refuge,
a mighty stronghold to save me;
for you are my rock, my stronghold.
Free me from the hand of the wicked.

3. It is you, O Lord, who are my hope,
my trust, O Lord, since my youth.
On you I have leaned from my birth,
from my mother's womb you have been my help.

4. My lips will tell of your justice
and day by day of your help.
O God, you have taught me from my youth
and I proclaim your wonders still.

SECOND READING
1 Corinthians 12:31, 13:13

There are three things that last; faith, hope and love; and the greatest of these is love.

Be ambitious for the higher gifts. And I am going to show you a way that is better than any of them.

If I have all the eloquence of men or of angels, but speak without love, I am simply a gong booming or a cymbal clashing. If I have the gift of prophecy, understanding all the mysteries there are, and knowing everything, and if I have faith in all its fullness, to move mountains, but without love, then I am nothing at all. If I give away all that I possess, piece by piece, and if I even let them take my body to burn it, but am without love, it will do me no good whatever.

Love is always patient and kind; it is never jealous; love is never boastful or conceited; it is never rude or selfish; it does not take offence, and is not resentful. Love takes no pleasure in other people's sins but delights in the truth; it is always ready to excuse, to trust, to hope, and to endure whatever comes.
Love does not come to an end. But if there are gifts of prophecy, the time will come when they must fail; or the gift of languages, it will not continue for ever; and knowledge—for this, too, the time will come when it must fail. For our knowledge is imperfect and our prophesying is imperfect; but once perfection comes, all imperfect things will disappear. When I was a child, I used to talk like a child, and think like a child, and argue like a child, but now I am a man, all childish ways are put behind me. Now we are seeing a dim reflection in a mirror; but then we shall be seeing face to face. The knowledge that I have now is imperfect; but then I shall know as fully as I am known.
In short, there are three things that last: faith, hope and love; and the greatest of these is love.
This is the word of the Lord. **Thanks be to God.**

All stand to greet the Gospel. If this Acclamation is not sung it may be omitted.
Alleluia, alleluia! I am the Way, the Truth and the Life, says the Lord; no one can come to the Father except through me. Alleluia!

THE GOSPEL   *Luke 4:21-30*
The Lord be with you. **And also with you.**
A reading from the holy Gospel according to Luke. **Glory to you, Lord.**
Like Elijah and Elisha, Jesus is not sent to the Jews only.
Jesus began to speak to them in the synagogue, "This text is being fulfilled today even as you listen." And he won the approval of all, and they were astonished by the gracious words that came from his lips.
They said, "This is Joseph's son, surely?" But he replied, "No doubt you will quote me the saying, 'Physician, heal yourself' and tell me, 'We have heard all that happened in Capernaum, do the same here in your own countryside.' " And he went on, "I tell you solemnly, no prophet is ever accepted in his own country.
"There were many widows in Israel, I can assure you, in Elijah's day, when heaven remained shut for three years and six months and a great famine raged throughout the land, but Elijah was not sent to any one of these: he was sent to a widow at Zarephath, a Sidonian town. And in the prophet Elisha's time there were many lepers in Israel, but none of these was cured, except the Syrian, Naaman."
When they heard this everyone in the synagogue was enraged. They sprang to their feet and hustled him out of the town; and they took him up to the brow of the hill their town was built on, intending to throw him down the cliff, but he slipped through the crowd and walked away.
This is the Gospel of the Lord. **Praise to you, Lord Jesus Christ.**

The Homily may follow, then Turn to page 6 for the Creed.

PRAYER OVER THE GIFTS

Lord, be pleased with the gifts we bring to your altar, and make them the sacrament of our salvation.	Lord, we have placed the gifts we owe you on your altar. In your mercy accept them, and make them the sacrament of our redemption.

Turn to pages 10 and 11 for the Sunday Prefaces

COMMUNION ANTIPHON

Let your face shine on your servant, and save me by your love. Lord, keep me from shame, for I have called to you.

Lord, look upon your servant: save me in your mercy. I have called upon you, do not let me be ashamed.

PRAYER AFTER COMMUNION

Lord,
you invigorate us with this help to our salvation.
By this eucharist give the true faith continued growth throughout the world.

Lord, you have given us the food which redeems us. May it help us on the way to everlasting salvation and make us ever more loyal in our faith.

Turn to page 25 for the Concluding Rite

5th Sunday of the Year

As the priest goes to the altar everyone joins in this Entrance Antiphon or a hymn.

Come, let us worship the Lord. Let us bow down in the presence of our maker, for he is the Lord our God.

Come, let us worship the Lord; let us pay homage to him who created us; for he is the Lord our God.

Turn to page 4

OPENING PRAYER

Father,
watch over your family
and keep us safe in your care,
for all our hope is in you.

Be faithful to your people, Lord, we pray, and do not cease to protect us. Guard us always and defend us, for we have no hope apart from your grace.

FIRST READING   *Isaiah 6:1–8*

Here I am, send me.

In the year of King Uzziah's death I saw the Lord seated on a high throne; his train filled the sanctuary; above him stood seraphs, each one with six wings.
And they cried out one to another in this way,
"Holy, holy, holy is the Lord of hosts.
His glory fills the whole earth."
The foundations of the threshold shook with the voice of the one who cried out, and the Temple was filled with smoke. I said:
"What a wretched state I am in! I am lost,
for I am a man of unclean lips
and I live among a people of unclean lips,
and my eyes have looked at the King, the Lord of hosts."
Then one of the seraphs flew to me, holding in his hand a live coal which he had taken from the altar with a pair of tongs. With this he touched my mouth and said:

"See now, this has touched your lips,
your sin is taken away,
your iniquity is purged."
Then I heard the voice of the Lord saying:
"Whom shall I send? Who will be our messenger?"
I answered, "Here I am, send me."
This is the word of the Lord. **Thanks be to God.**

RESPONSORIAL PSALM   *Psalm 137*
Before the angels I will bless you, O Lord.

1. I thank you, Lord, with all my heart,
you have heard the words of my mouth.
Before the angels I will bless you.
I will adore before your holy temple.

2. I thank you for your faithfulness and
   love
which excel all we ever knew of you.
On the day I called, you answered;
you increased the strength of my soul.

3. All earth's kings shall thank you
when they hear the words of your
   mouth.
They shall sing of the Lord's ways:
"How great is the glory of the Lord!"

4. You stretch out your hand and save
   me,
your hand will do all things for me.
Your love, O Lord, is eternal,
discard not the work of your hands.

SECOND READING   *1 Corinthians 15:1-11*
I preach what they preach, and this is what you all believed.

Brothers, I want to remind you of the gospel I preached to you, the gospel that you
received and in which you are firmly established; because the gospel will save you
only if you keep believing exactly what I preached to you—believing anything else
will not lead to anything.
Well then in the first place, I taught you what I had been taught myself, namely that
Christ died for our sins, in accordance with the scriptures; that he was buried; and
that he was raised to life on the third day, in accordance with the scriptures; that he
appeared first to Cephas and secondly to the Twelve. Next he appeared to more than
five hundred of the brothers at the same time, most of whom are still alive, though
some have died; then he appeared to James, and then to all the apostles; and last of
all he appeared to me too; it was as though I was born when no one expected it.
I am the least of the apostles; in fact, since I persecuted the Church of God, I hardly
deserve the name apostle; but by God's grace that is what I am, and the grace that he
gave me has not been fruitless. On the contrary, I, or rather the grace of God that is
with me, have worked harder than any of the others; but what matters is that I
preach what they preach, and this is what you all believed.
This is the word of the Lord. **Thanks be to God.**

All stand to greet the Gospel. If this Acclamation is not sung it may be omitted.
Alleluia, alleluia!
I call you friends, says the Lord,
because I have made known to you
everything I have learnt from my Father.
Alleluia!

THE GOSPEL *Luke 5:1-11*
The Lord be with you. **And also with you.**
A reading from the holy Gospel according to Luke.
They left everything and followed him.
Jesus was standing one day by the lake of Gennesaret, with the crowd pressing round him listening to the word of God, when he caught sight of two boats close to the bank. The fishermen had gone out of them and were washing their nets. He got into one of the boats—it was Simon's—and asked him to put out a little from the shore. Then he sat down and taught the crowds from the boat.
When he had finished speaking he said to Simon, "Put out into deep water and pay out your nets for a catch." "Master," Simon replied, "we worked hard all night long and caught nothing, but if you say so, I will pay out the nets." And when they had done this they netted such a huge number of fish that their nets began to tear, so they signalled to their companions in the other boat to come and help them; when these came, they filled the two boats to sinking point.
When Simon Peter saw this he fell at the knees of Jesus saying, "Leave me, Lord; I am a sinful man." For he and all his companions were completely overcome by the catch they had made; so also were James and John, sons of Zebedee, who were Simon's partners. But Jesus said to Simon, "Do not be afraid; from now on it is men you will catch." Then, bringing their boats back to land, they left everything and followed him.
This is the Gospel of the Lord. **Praise to you, Lord Jesus Christ.**

The Homily may follow, then Turn to page 6 for the Creed.

PRAYER OVER THE GIFTS
Lord our God,
may the bread and wine
you give us for our nourishment on earth
become the sacrament of our eternal life.

Lord, our God, you made this bread and wine to support us in our weakness. Grant that they may become the sacrament which brings us eternal life.

Turn to pages 10 and 11 for the Sunday Prefaces

COMMUNION ANTIPHON
Give praise to the Lord for his kindness, for his wonderful deeds towards men. He has filled the hungry with good things, he has satisfied the thirsty.

Let us thank the Lord for his compassion and the wonderful things he has done for us;
He has refreshed all who are thirsty, and taken their hunger away.

PRAYER AFTER COMMUNION
God our Father,
you give us a share in the one bread and the one cup
and make us one in Christ.
Help us to bring your salvation and joy to all the world.

O God, you have given us one Bread and one Chalice to share. We ask you therefore, that we may find our joy in living as one in Christ, and so contributing to the salvation of the world.

Turn to page 25 for the Concluding Rite

6th Sunday of the Year

As the priest goes to the altar everyone joins in this Entrance Antiphon or a hymn.

Lord, be my rock of safety, the stronghold that saves me. For the honour of your name, lead me and guide me.

O God, be my protector, be a stronghold to keep me safe; you are my rock and my refuge; be true to your holy Name; lead me and care for me.

Turn to page 4

OPENING PRAYER

God our Father,
you have promised to remain for ever
with those who do what is just and right.
Help us to live in your presence.

Lord, you promise to make your home
in upright and sincere hearts. Give us
the grace to make ourselves worthy
dwelling-places for you.

FIRST READING
Jeremiah 17:5-8

A curse on the man who puts his trust in man, a blessing on the man who puts his trust in the Lord.

The Lord says this: "A curse on the man who puts his trust in man, who relies on things of flesh, whose heart turns from the Lord. He is like dry scrub in the wastelands: if good comes, he has no eyes for it, he settles in the parched places of the wilderness, a salt land, uninhabited.

"A blessing on the man who puts his trust in the Lord, with the Lord for his hope. He is like a tree by the waterside that thrusts its roots to the stream: when the heat comes it feels no alarm, its foliage stays green; it has no worries in a year of drought, and never ceases to bear fruit."

This the word of the Lord. **Thanks be to God.**

RESPONSORIAL PSALM
Psalm 1

Happy the man who has placed his trust in the Lord.

1. Happy indeed is the man
who follows not the counsel of the
   wicked;
nor lingers in the way of sinners
nor sits in the company of scorners,
but whose delight is the law of the Lord
and who ponders his law day and night.

2. He is like a tree that is planted
beside the flowing waters,
that yields its fruit in due season
and whose leaves shall never fade;
and all that he does shall prosper.

3. Not so are the wicked, not so!
For they like winnowed chaff
shall be driven away by the wind.
For the Lord guards the way of the just
but the way of the wicked leads to doom.

SECOND READING
1 Corinthians 15:12, 16-20

If Christ has not been raised, your believing is useless.

If Christ raised from the dead is what has been preached, how can some of you be saying that there is no resurrection of the dead? For if the dead are not raised, Christ has not been raised, and if Christ has not been raised, you are still in your sins. And what is more serious, all who have died in Christ have perished. If our hope in Christ has been for this life only, we are the most unfortunate of all people.

But Christ has in fact been raised from the dead, the first-fruits of all who have fallen asleep.
This is the word of the Lord. **Thanks be to God.**

All stand to greet the Gospel. If this Acclamation is not sung it may be omitted.
Alleluia, alleluia! Blessed are you, Father, Lord of heaven and earth, for revealing the mysteries of the kingdom to mere children. Alleluia!

THE GOSPEL *Luke 6:17, 20-26*

The Lord be with you. **And also with you.**
A reading from the holy Gospel according to Luke. **Glory to you Lord.**
How happy are you who are poor. Alas for you who are rich.

Jesus came down with the Twelve and stopped at a piece of level ground where there was a large gathering of his disciples with a great crowd of people from all parts of Judaea and from Jerusalem and from the coastal region of Tyre and Sidon who had come to hear him and to be cured of their diseases.

Then fixing his eyes on his disciples he said: "How happy are you who are poor: yours is the kingdom of God. Happy you who are hungry now: you shall be satisfied. Happy you who weep now: you shall laugh.

"Happy are you when people hate you, drive you out, abuse you, denounce your name as criminal, on account of the Son of Man. Rejoice when that day comes and dance for joy, for then your reward will be great in heaven. This was the way their ancestors treated the prophets.

"But alas for you who are rich: you are having your consolation now. Alas for you who have your fill now: you shall go hungry. Alas for you who laugh now: you shall mourn and weep.

"Alas for you when the world speaks well of you! This was the way their ancestors treated the false prophets."

This is the Gospel of the Lord. **Praise to you, Lord Jesus Christ.**

The Homily may follow, then Turn to page 6 for the Creed.

PRAYER OVER THE GIFTS

Lord,
we make this offering in obedience to your word.
May it cleanse and renew us,
and lead us to our eternal reward.

May this offering, Lord, purify us and renew us, so that we may be enabled to do your will and gain everlasting reward.

Turn to pages 10 and 11 for the Sunday Prefaces

COMMUNION ANTIPHON

They ate and were filled; the Lord gave them what they wanted: they were not deprived of their desire.

The people have eaten and been satisfied; the Lord has given them what they desired; they have not been disappointed.

PRAYER AFTER COMMUNION

Lord,
you give us food from heaven.
May we always hunger
for the bread of life.

You have given us, Lord the food of heaven for out delight. Grant us the grace to seek this food always, for without it we cannot truly live.

Turn to page 25 for the Concluding Rite

64

7th Sunday of the Year

As the priest goes to the altar everyone joins in this Entrance Antiphon or hymn.

Lord, your mercy is my hope, my heart rejoices in your saving power. I will sing to the Lord for his goodness to me.

Turn to page 4

OPENING PRAYER

Father,
keep before us the wisdom and love
you have revealed in your Son.
Help us to be like him
in word and deed,
for he lives and reigns with you and the
Holy Spirit,
one God, for ever and ever.

I have placed all my hope in your mercy, Lord;
my heart has rejoiced in your salvation.
I shall sing to the Lord because he has been good to me.

Grant us the grace, almighty God, always to keep your truth in our hearts, so that every word we speak and every action we perform may be in accordance with your will.

FIRST READING   *1 Samuel 26:2.7-9, 12-13, 22-23*

The Lord put you in my power, but I would not raise my hand.

Saul set off and went down to the wilderness of Ziph, accompanied by three thousand men chosen from Israel to search for David in the wilderness of Ziph.
So in the dark David and Abishai made their way towards the force, where they found Saul asleep inside the camp, his spear stuck in the ground beside his head, with Abner and the troops lying round him.
Then Abishai said to David, "Today God has put your enemy in your power; so now let me pin him to the ground with his own spear. Just one stroke! I will not need to strike him twice." David answered Abishai, "Do not kill him, for who can lift his hand against the Lord's anointed and be without guilt?" David took the spear and the pitcher of water from beside Saul's head, and they made off. No one saw, no one knew, no one woke up; they were all asleep, for a deep sleep from the Lord had fallen on them.
David crossed to the other side and halted on the top of the mountain a long way off; there was a wide space between them. David then called out, "Here is the king's spear. Let one of the soldiers come across and take it. The Lord repays everyone for his uprightness and loyalty. Today the Lord put you in my power, but I would not raise my hand against the Lord's anointed."
This is the word of the Lord. **Thanks be to God.**

RESPONSORIAL PSALM   *Psalm 102*
The Lord is compassion and love.

1. My soul, give thanks to the Lord,
all my being, bless his holy name.
My soul, give thanks to the Lord
and never forget all his blessings.

2. It is he who forgives all your guilt,
who heals every one of your ills,
who redeems your life from the grave,
who crowns you with love and
compassion.

3. The Lord is compassion and love,
slow to anger and rich in mercy.
He does not treat us according to our
sins
nor repay us according to our faults.

4. As far as the east is from the west
so far does he remove our sins.
As a father has compassion on his sons,
the Lord has pity on those who fear him.

SECOND READING   *1 Corinthians 15:45-49*
We who have been modelled on the earthly man will be modelled on the heavenly
mana.
The first man, Adam, as scripture says, became a living soul; but the last Adam has
become a life-giving spirit. That is first the one with the soul, not the spirit, and after
that, the one with the spirit. The first man, being from the earth, is earthly by nature;
the second man is from heaven. As this earthly man was, so are we on earth; and as
the heavenly man is, so are we in heaven. And we, who have been modelled on the
earthly man, will be modelled on the heavenly man.
This is the word of the Lord. **Thanks be to God.**
All stand to greet the Gospel. If this Acclamation is not sung it may be omitted.
Alleluia, alleluia! Open our heart, O Lord, to accept the words of your Son. Alleluia!

THE GOSPEL   *Luke 6:27-38*
The Lord be with you. **And also with you.**
A reading from the holy Gospel according to Luke. **Glory to you Lord.**
Be compassionate as your Father is compassionate.

Jesus said to his disciples: "But I say this to you who are listening: Love your
enemies, do good to those who hate you, bless those who curse you, pray for those
who treat you badly. To the man who slaps you on one cheek, present the other
cheek too; to the man who takes your cloak from you, do not refuse your tunic. Give
to everyone who asks you, and do not ask for your property back from the man who
robs you. Treat others as you would like them to treat you. If you love those who
love you, what thanks can you expect? Even sinners love those who love them. And
if you do good to those who do good to you, what thanks can you expect? For even
sinners do that much. And if you lend to those from whom you hope to receive, what
thanks can you expect? Even sinners lend to sinners to get back the same amount.
Instead, love your enemies and do good, and lend without any hope of return. You
will have a great reward, and you will be sons of the Most High, for he himself is
kind to the ungrateful and the wicked.
"Be compassionate as your Father is compassionate. Do not judge, and you will
not be judged yourselves; do not condemn, and you will not be condemned
yourselves; grant pardon, and you will be pardoned. Give, and there will be gifts for
you: a full measure, pressed down, shaken together, and running over, will be
poured into your lap; because the amount you measure out is the amount you will
be given back."
This is the Gospel of the Lord. **Praise to you Lord Jesus Christ.**

The Homily may follow, then Turn to page 6 for the Creed.

PRAYER OVER THE GIFTS
Lord,   Lord, we celebrate this sacrifice to pay
as we make this offering,   you our debt of worship. Grant that this
may our worship in Spirit and truth   offering may help us to obtain salvation.
bring us salvation.

Turn to pages 10 and 11 for the Sunday Prefaces

COMMUNION ANTIPHON

I will tell all your marvellous works. I will rejoice and be glad in you, and sing to your name, Most High.

I will proclaim all your wonders, you will be my joy;
I will sing your praises, O Lord most High.

PRAYER AFTER COMMUNION

Almighty God,
help us to live the example of love
we celebrate in this eucharist, that we
may come to its fulfilment in your
  presence.

We have received, Lord, in this sacrament the pledge of our salvation. Grant, we pray, that we may also receive its fulfilment.

Turn to page 25 for the Concluding Rite

8th Sunday of the Year

As the priest goes to the altar everyone joins in this Entrance Antiphon or hymn.

The Lord has been my strength; he has led me into freedom. He saved me because he loves me.

The Lord has shown himself my protector:
he has rescued me and set me free, because he has loved me.

Turn to page 4

OPENING PRAYER

Lord,
guide the course of world events
and give your Church the joy and peace
of serving you in freedom.

Grant, Lord, that the world may follow guidance in peace, and the church may rejoice in the freedom to do your will.

FIRST READING   Ecclesiasticus 27: 1-7

Do not praise a man before he has spoken.

In a shaken sieve the rubbish is left behind, so too the defects of a man appear in his talk. The kiln tests the work of the potter, the test of a man is in his conversation. The orchard where the tree grows is judged on the quality of its fruit, similarly a man's words betray what he feels. Do not praise a man before he has spoken, since this is the test of men.

This is the word of the Lord. Thanks be to God.

RESPONSORIAL PSALM   Psalm 91

It is good to give you thanks, O Lord.

1. It is good to give thanks to the Lord
to make music to your name, O Most High,
to proclaim your love in the morning
and your truth in the watches of the night.

2. The just will flourish like the palmtree
and grow like a Lebanon cedar.

3. Planted in the house of the Lord
they will flourish in the courts of our God,
still bearing fruit when they are old,
still full of sap, still green.
In him, my rock, there is no wrong.

SECOND READING   *I Corinthians 15 : 54-58*
He has given us the victory through our Lord Jesus Christ.

When this perishable nature has put on imperishability, and when this mortal
nature has put on immortality, then the words of scripture will come true: Death is
swallowed up in victory. Death, where is your victory? Death, where is your sting?
Now the sting of death is sin, and sin gets its power from the Law. So let us thank
God for giving us the victory through our Lord Jesus Christ.
Never give in then, my dear brothers, never admit defeat; keep on working at the
Lord's work always, knowing that, in the Lord, you cannot be labouring in vain.
This is the word of the Lord. **Thanks be to God.**
All stand to greet the Gospel. If this Acclamation is not sung it may be omitted.
Alleluia, alleluia! Open our heart, O Lord, to accept the words of your Son. Alleluia!

THE GOSPEL   *Luke 6 :39-45*
The Lord be with you. **And also with you.**
A reading from the holy Gospel according to Luke. **Glory to you, Lord.**
A man's words flow out of what fills his heart.

Jesus told a parable to them, "Can one blind man guide another? Surely both will
fall into a pit? The disciple is not superior to his teacher; the fully trained disciple
will always be like his teacher. Why do you observe the splinter in your brother's eye
and never notice the plank in your own? How can you say to your brother, 'Brother
let me take out the splinter that is in your eye,' when you cannot see the plank in your
own? Hyprocrite! Take the plank out of your own eye first, and then you will see
clearly enough to take out the splinter that is in your brother's eye.
"There is no sound tree that produces rotten fruit, nor again a rotten tree that
produces sound fruit. For every tree can be told by its own fruit: people do not pick
figs from thorns, nor gather grapes from brambles. A good man draws what is good
from the store of goodness in his heart; a bad man draws what is bad from the store
of badness. For a man's words flow out of what fills his heart."
This is the Gospel of the Lord. **Praise to you, Lord Jesus Christ.**

The Homily may follow, then Turn to page 6 for the Creed.

PRAYER OVER THE GIFTS
God our Creator,
may this bread and wine we offer
as a sign of our love and worship
lead us to salvation.

O God, we have nothing but your own
gifts to offer you, yet you accept them as
a token of our loving worship. Grant us
the grace we need to make us worthy of
receiving our eternal reward.

Turn to pages 10 and 11 for the Sunday Prefaces

COMMUNION ANTIPHON
**I will sing to the Lord for his goodness to
me, I will sing the name of the Lord, Most
High.**

**I will praise the Lord for he has been
good to me,
and sing in honour of the Lord most High.**

PRAYER AFTER COMMUNION

God of salvation,
may this sacrament which strengthens
us here on earth
bring us to eternal life.

You have given us, Lord, your sacrament to strengthen us in this life. Grant that it may enable us to share in the life that never ends.

Turn to page 25 for the Concluding Rite

Ash Wednesday

As the priest goes to the altar everyone joins in this Entrance Antiphon or a hymn.

Lord, you are merciful to all, and hate nothing you have created. You overlook the sins of men to bring them to repentence. You are the Lord our God.

**You are merciful to all men, Lord; you love all your creatures.
When we repent, you forget our sins and spare us,
for you are the Lord our God.**

The Penitential Rite and the Gloria are omitted.

OPENING PRAYER

Lord,
protect us in our struggle against evil.
As we begin the discipline of Lent,
make this season holy by our self-denial.

Lord, our struggle is against the forces of evil. Grant that during this Lent we may submit to rigorous training and learn self-control through the fast with which we begin this season.

FIRST READING   *Joel 2:12-18*

Let your hearts be broken, not your garments torn.

"But now, now—it is the Lord who speaks—come back to me with all your heart, fasting, weeping, mourning." Let your hearts be broken, not your garments torn, turn to the Lord your God again, for he is all tenderness and compassion, slow to anger, rich in graciousness, and ready to relent. Who knows if he will not turn again, will not relent, will not leave a blessing as he passes, oblation and libation for the Lord your God? Sound the trumpet in Zion! Order a fast, proclaim a solemn assembly, call the people together, summon the community, assemble the elders, gather the children, even the infants at the breast. Let the bridegroom leave his bedroom and the bride her alcove. Between vestibule and altar let the priests, the ministers of the Lord, lament. Let them say, "Spare your people, Lord! Do not make your heritage a thing of shame, a byword for the nations. Why should it be said among the nations, 'Where is their God?' " Then the Lord, jealous on behalf of his land, took pity on his people.
This is the word of the Lord. **Thanks be to God.**

RESPONSORIAL PSALM   *Psalm 50*
Have mercy on us, O Lord, for we have sinned.

1. Have mercy on me, God, in your
   kindness.
In your compassion blot out my offence.
O wash me more and more from my
   guilt
and cleanse me from my sin.

2. My offences truly I know them;
my sin is always before me.
Against you, you alone, have I sinned:
what is evil in your sight I have done.

3. A pure heart create for me, O God,
put a steadfast spirit within me.
Do not cast me away from your
   presence,
nor deprive me of your holy spirit.

4. Give me again the joy of your help;
with the spirit of fervour sustain me,
O Lord, open my lips
and my mouth shall declare your praise.

SECOND READING   *2 Corinthians 5:20-6:2*
Be reconciled to God . . . now is the favourable time.
We are ambassadors for Christ; it is as though God were appealing through us, and
the appeal that we make in Christ's name is: be reconciled to God. For our sake God
made the sinless one into sin, so that in him we might become the goodness of God.
As his fellow workers, we beg you once again not to neglect the grace of God that
you have received. For he says: At the favourable time, I have listened to you; on the
day of salvation I came to your help. Well, now is the favourable time; this is the day
of salvation.
This is the word of the Lord. **Thanks be to God.**
All stand to greet the Gospel. If this Acclamation is not sung it may be omitted.
A pure heart create for me, O God, and give me again the joy of your help.

THE GOSPEL   *Matthew 6:1-6, 16-18*
The Lord be with you. **And also with you.**
A reading from the holy Gospel according to Matthew. **Glory to you, Lord.**
Your Father who sees all that is done in secret will reward you.

Jesus said to his disciples: "Be careful not to parade your good deeds before men to
attract their notice; by doing this you will lose all reward from your Father in
heaven. So when you give alms, do not have it trumpeted before you; this is what the
hypocrites do in the synagogues and in the streets to win men's admiration. I tell you
solemnly, they have had their reward. But when you give alms, your left hand must
not know what your right is doing; your almsgiving must be secret, and your Father
who sees all that is done in secret will reward you.
"And when you pray, do not imitate the hypocrites: they love to say their prayers
standing up in the synagogues and at the street corners for people to see them. I tell
you solemnly, they have had their reward. But when you pray, go to your private
room and, when you have shut your door, pray to your Father who is in that secret
place, and your Father who sees all that is done in secret will reward you.
"When you fast do not put on a gloomy look as the hyprocrites do: they pull long
faces to let men know they are fasting. I tell you solemnly, they have had their
reward. But when you fast, put oil on your head and wash your face, so that no one
will know you are fasting except your Father who sees all that is done in secret; and
your Father who sees all that is done in secret will reward you."
This is the Gospel of the Lord. **Praise to you, Lord Jesus Christ.**
The Homily may follow.

THE BLESSING OF ASHES

Dear friends in Christ,
let us ask our Father
to bless these ashes
which we will use
as the mark of our repentence.

My dear people: As a sign of repentance
we shall put these ashes on our heads.
Let us ask God our Father to bless them
with his abundant grace.

All pray silently.

Lord,
bless the sinner who asks for your
   forgiveness
and bless + all those who receive these
   ashes.
May they keep this lenten season
in preparation for the joy of Easter.

O God, we know that you are moved to
mercy when we do penance in preparation for our sins. Listen then to our
prayers and bless + your servants as
they are sprinkled with these ashes.
Make us faithful to the observance of
Lent, so that we may come with hearts
made clean to celebrate the death and
resurrection of your Son.

*The priest sprinkles the ashes with holy water. He then places the ashes on those who
come forward, saying:*

Turn away from sin and be faithful to
   the gospel.

Repent, and believe the Gospel.

or

Remember, men, you are dust
and to dust you will return.

or

Remember, man, that you are dust
and to dust you shall return.

The following antiphons may be said, or a hymn sung.

1. Come back to the Lord with all
   your heart;
leave the past in ashes,
and turn to God with tears and fasting,
for he is slow to anger and ready to
   forgive.

2. Let the priests and ministers of the
   Lord
lament before his altar, and say:
Spare us, Lord; spare your people!
Do not let us die for we are crying
   out to you.

1. While we put on garments of
   penance,
while we fast and are sprinkled with
   ashes,
let us cry out to the Lord our God,
who in his mercy will forgive us our sins

2. Let the priests, the ministers of the
   Lord,
stand before the sanctuary and cry out:
Spare, O Lord, spare your people,
do not silence the lips that praise you.

There is no creed. Turn to page 7 for the Offertory Prayers

PRAYER OVER THE GIFTS

Lord,
help us to resist temptation
by our lenten works of charity and
   penance.
By this sacrifice
may we be prepared to celebrate
the death and resurrection of Christ our
   Saviour
and be cleansed from sin and renewed in
   spirit.

Lord as we offer you this sacrifice at the
beginning of Lent, we ask of you this
grace: grant that our works of penance
and charity may help us to overcome
our evil inclinations. Free us from our
sins, so that we may come worthily to
celebrate the Passion of your Son: who
lives and reigns for ever and ever.

Turn to page 8 for the Preface

COMMUNION ANTIPHON

**The man who meditates day and night on
the law of the Lord will yield fruit in due
season.**

**The man who ponders God's law by
   night and day
will bear fruit in due season.**

PRAYER AFTER COMMUNION

Lord,
through this communion
may our lenten penance give you glory
and bring us your protection.

May this sacrament, Lord, which we
have received, help us faithfully to
observe our fast in your honour, and so
be cured of our infirmities.

Turn to page 25 for the Concluding Rite

1st Sunday of Lent

As the priest goes to the altar everyone joins in this Entrance Antiphon or a hymn.

**When he calls to me, I will answer: I will
rescue him and give him honour. Long life
and contentment will be his.**

**He will call to me and I shall hear him;
I shall rescue him and give him glory,
and grant him length of days.**

Turn to page 4

OPENING PRAYER

Father,
through our observance of Lent,
help us to understand the meaning
of your Son's death and resurrection,
and teach us to reflect it in our lives.

Almighty God, grant that our annual
Lenten observance may help us to
penetrate more deeply into the mystery
of Christ, and through living holy lives
to grow in grace.

FIRST READING

Deuteronomy 26:4-10

The creed of the chosen people.

Moses said to the people: "The priest shall take the pannier from your hand and lay
it before the altar of the Lord your God. Then, in the sight of the Lord your God,
you must make this pronouncement:
'My father was a wandering Aramaean. He went down into Egypt to find refuge
there, few in numbers; but there he became a nation, great, mighty, and strong. The
Egyptians ill-treated us, they gave us no peace and inflicted harsh slavery on us. But

we called on the Lord, the God of our fathers. The Lord heard our voice and saw our misery, our toil and our oppression; and the Lord brought us out of Egypt with mighty hand and outstretched arm, with great terror, and with signs and wonders. he brought us here and gave us this land, a land where milk and honey flow. Here then I bring the first-fruits of the produce of the soil that you, Lord, have given me.' You must then lay them before the Lord your God, and bow down in the sight of the Lord your God."

This is the word of the Lord. **Thanks be to God.**

RESPONSORIAL PSALM   *Psalm 90*
Be with me, O Lord, in my distress.

1. He who dwells in the shelter of the Most High
and abides in the shade of the Almighty
says to the Lord: "My refuge,
my stronghold, my God in whom I trust!"

2. Upon you no evil shall fall,
no plague approach where you dwell.
For you has he commanded his angels,
to keep you in all your ways.

3. They shall bear you upon their hands
lest you strike your foot against a stone.
On the lion and the viper you will tread
and trample the young lion and the dragon.

4. His love he set on me, so I will rescue him;
protect him for he knows my name.
When he calls I shall answer: "I am with you."
I will save him in distress and give him glory.

SECOND READING   *Romans 10:8-13*
The creed of the Christian.

Scripture says: The word, that is the faith we proclaim, is very near to you, it is on your lips and in your heart. If your lips confess that Jesus is Lord and if you believe in your heart that God raised him from the dead, then you will be saved. By believing from the heart you are made righteous; by confessing with your lips you are saved. When scripture says: those who believe in him will have no cause for shame, it makes no distinction between Jew and Greek: all belong to the same Lord who is rich enough, however many ask for his help, for everyone who calls on the name of the Lord will be saved.

This is the word of the Lord. **Thanks be to God.**

All stand to greet the Gospel. If this Acclamation is not sung it may be ommitted.
Man does not live on bread alone, but on every word that comes from the mouth of God.

THE GOSPEL   *Luke 4:1-13*

The Lord be with you. **And also with you.**
A reading from the holy Gospel according to Luke. **Glory to you, Lord.**

Jesus was led by the Spirit through the wilderness and was tempted there.

Filled with the Holy Spirit, Jesus left the Jordan and was led by the Spirit through the wilderness, being tempted there by the devil for forty days. During that time he ate nothing and at the end he was hungry. Then the devil said to him, "If you are the Son of God, tell this stone to turn into a loaf." But Jesus replied, "Scripture says: Man does not live on bread alone."

Then leading him to a height, the devil showed him in a moment of time all the kingdoms of the world and said to him, "I will give you all this power and the glory of these kingdoms, for it has been committed to me and I give it to anyone I choose. Worship me, then, and it shall all be yours." But Jesus answered him, "Scripture says:

You must worship the Lord your God, and serve him alone."
Then he led him to Jerusalem and made him stand on the parapet of the Temple.
"If you are the Son of God," he said to him "throw yourself down from here, for scripture says: He will put his angels in charge of you to guard you, and again: They will hold you up on their hands in case you hurt your foot against a stone." But Jesus answered him, "It has been said: You must not put the Lord Your God to the test." Having exhausted all these ways of tempting him, the devil left him, to return at the appointed time.
This is the Gospel of the Lord. **Praise to you, Lord Jesus Christ.**

The Homily may follow, then Turn to page 6 for the Creed.

PRAYER OVER THE GIFTS

Lord,
make us worthy to bring you these gifts.
May this sacrifice
help to change our lives.

We pray you, almighty God, make us fit to offer these gifts, by which we celebrate the beginning of the holy season of Lent.

Turn to page 12 for the Lent Prefaces

COMMUNION ANTIPHON

Man does not live on bread alone, but on every word that comes from the mouth of God.

Man does not live by bread alone, but by every word that comes from the mouth of God.

PRAYER AFTER COMMUNION
Father,
you increase our faith and hope,
you deepen our love in this communion.
Help us to live by your words
and to seek Christ, our bread of life,
who is Lord for ever and ever.

You have refreshed us, Lord, with the Bread of Heaven, which nourishes our faith enlarges our hope and strengthens our charity. Teach us to hunger after the true bread of life, so that we may learn to live by every word that comes from your mouth.

Turn to page 25 for the Concluding Rite

2nd Sunday of Lent

As the priest goes to the altar everyone joins in this Entrance Antiphon or a hymn.

Remember your mercies, Lord, your tenderness from ages past. Do not let our enemies triumph over us; O God, deliver Israel from all her distress.

Lord, remember your everlasting kindness and mercy; never let our enemies prevail over us; God of Israel, rescue us when we are in trouble.

Turn to page 4

OPENING PRAYER

God our Father,
help us to hear your Son.
Enlighten us with your word,
that we may find the way to your glory.

O God, you commanded us to listen to your beloved Son. Nourish our minds with your gospel and clarify our vision, so that we may rejoice in the contemplation of your glory in heaven.

FIRST READING   *Genesis 15:5-12, 17-18*

God enters into a Covenant with Abraham, the man of faith.

Taking Abram outside the Lord said, "Look up to heaven and count the stars if you can. Such will be your descendants" he told him. Abram put his faith in the Lord, who counted this as making him justified.

"I am the Lord" he said to him "who brought you out of Ur of the Chaldaeans to make you heir to this land." "My Lord, the Lord" Abram replied "how am I to know that I shall inherit it?" He said to him, "Get me a three-year-old heifer, a three-year-old goat, a three-year-old ram, a turtledove and a young pigeon." He brought him all these, cut them in half and put half on one side and half facing it on the other; but the birds he did not cut in half. Birds of prey came down on the carcasses but Abram drove them off.

Now as the sun was setting Abram fell into a deep sleep, and terror seized him. When the sun had set and darkness had fallen, there appeared a smoking furnace and a fire-brand that went between the halves. That day the Lord made a Covenant with Abram in these terms:

"To your descendants I give this land, from the wadi of Egypt to the Great River." This is the word of the Lord. **Thanks be to God.**

RESPONSORIAL PSALM   *Psalm 26*

The Lord is my light and my help.

1. The Lord is my light and my help;
whom shall I fear?
The Lord is the stronghold of my life;
before whom shall I shrink?

2. O Lord, hear my voice when I call;
have mercy and answer.
Of you my heart has spoken:
"Seek his face."

3. It is your face, O Lord, that I seek;
hide not your face.
Dismiss not your servant in anger;
you have been my help.

4. I am sure I shall see the Lord's goodness
in the land of the living.
Hope in him, hold firm and take heart.
Hope in the Lord!

SECOND READING   *Philippians 3:17-4:1*

Christ will transfigure our bodies into copies of his glorious body.

My brothers, be united in following my rule of life. Take as your models everybody who is already doing this and study them as you used to study us. I have told you often, and I repeat it today with tears, there are many who are behaving as the enemies of the cross of Christ. They are destined to be lost. They make foods into their god and they are proudest of something they ought to think shameful; the things they think important are earthly things.

For us, our homeland is in heaven, and from heaven comes the saviour we are waiting for, the Lord Jesus Christ, and he will transfigure these wretched bodies of ours into copies of his glorious body. He will do that by the same power with which he can subdue the whole universe.

So then, my brothers and dear friends, do not give way but remain faithful in the Lord. I miss you very much, dear friends; you are my joy and my crown. This is the word of the Lord. **Thanks be to God.**

All stand to greet the Gospel. If this Acclamation is not sung it may be omitted.
From the bright cloud the Father's voice was heard: "This is my Son, the beloved. Listen to him."

THE GOSPEL *Luke 9:28-36*

The Lord be with you. **And also with you.**
A reading from the holy Gospel according to Luke. **Glory to you, Lord.**
As Jesus prayed, the aspect of his face was changed.
Jesus took with him Peter and John and James and went up the mountain to pray. As he prayed, the aspect of his face was changed and his clothing became brilliant as lightning. Suddenly there were two men there talking to him; they were Moses and Elijah appearing in glory, and they were speaking of his passing which he was to accomplish in Jerusalem. Peter and his companions were heavy with sleep, but they kept awake and saw his glory and the two men standing with him. As these were leaving him, Peter said to Jesus, "Master, it is wonderful for us to be here; so let us make three tents, one for you one for Moses and one for Elijah."—He did not know what he was saying. As he spoke, a cloud came and covered them with shadow; and when they went into the cloud the disciples were afraid. And a voice came from the cloud saying, "This is my Son, the Chosen One. Listen to him." And after the voice had spoken, Jesus was found alone. The disciples kept silence and, at that time, told no one what they had seen.
This is the Gospel of the Lord. **Praise to you, Lord Jesus Christ.**

The Homily may follow, then Turn to page 6 for the Creed.

PRAYER OVER THE GIFTS
Lord,
make us holy.
May this eucharist take away our sins
that we may be prepared
to celebrate the resurrection.

May this sacrifice, Lord, wash away our
sins, and make us holy in body and soul
for the celebration of Easter.

Turn to page 12 for the Lent Prefaces

COMMUNION ANTIPHON
This is my Son, my beloved, in whom is all my delight: listen to him.

**This is my beloved Son with whom I am
well pleased;
listen to him!**

PRAYER AFTER COMMUNION
Lord,
we give thanks for these holy mysteries
which bring to us here on earth
a share in the life to come,
through Christ our Lord.

We are filled with thankfulness, Lord,
for the glorious sacrament we have
received, by which, while we are still on
earth, you grant us a taste of heaven.

Turn to page 25 for the Concluding Rite

3rd Sunday of Lent

As the priest goes to the altar everyone joins in this Entrance Antiphon or a hymn.

My eyes are ever fixed on the Lord, for he releases my feet from the snare. O look at me and be merciful, for I am wretched and alone.

**My eyes are always on the Lord,
for he will free my feet from the snare.
Turn to me and have mercy,
for I am lonely and poor.**

Turn to page 4

OPENING PRAYER

Father,
you have taught us to overcome our sins by prayer, fasting and works of mercy. When we are discouraged by our weakness,
give us confidence in your love.

O God, source of all mercy and goodness, you have taught us to find the remedy for our sins in fasting, prayer and almsgiving. Receive our humble confession of our faults, and in your mercy take away the guilt that weighs upon our consciences.

FIRST READING

Exodus 3:1-8, 13-15

I Am has sent me to you.

Moses was looking after the flock of Jethro, his father-in-law, priest of Midian. He led his flock to the far side of the wilderness and came to Horeb, the mountain of God. There the angel of the Lord appeared to him in the shape of a flame of fire, coming from the middle of a bush. Moses looked; there was the bush blazing but it was not being burnt up. "I must go and look at this strange sight," Moses said "and see why the bush is not burnt." Now the Lord saw him go forward to look, and God called to him from the middle of the bush. "Moses, Moses!" he said. "Here I am" he answered. "Come no nearer" he said. "Take off your shoes, for the place on which you stand is holy ground. I am the God of your father," he said "the God of Abraham, the God of Isaac and the God of Jacob." At this Moses covered his face, afraid to look at God.

And the Lord said, "I have seen the miserable state of my people in Egypt. I have heard their appeal to be free of their slave-drivers. Yes, I am well aware of their sufferings. I mean to deliver them out of the hands of the Egyptians and bring them up out of that land to a land rich and broad, a land where milk and honey flow."

Then Moses said to God, "I am to go, then, to the sons of Israel and say to them, 'The God of your fathers has sent me to you.' But if they ask me what his name is, what am I to tell them?" And God said to Moses, "I Am who I Am. This" he added "is what you must say to the sons of Israel: 'I Am has sent me to you.' " And God also said to Moses, "You are to say to the sons of Israel: 'The Lord, the God of your fathers, the God of Abraham, the God of Isaac, and the God of Jacob, has sent me to you.' This is my name for all time; by this name I shall be invoked for all generations to come."

This is the word of the Lord. **Thanks be to God.**

RESPONSORIAL PSALM

Psalm 102

The Lord is compassion and love.

1. My soul, give thanks to the Lord,
all my being, bless his holy name.
My soul give thanks to the Lord
and never forget all his blessings.

2. It is he who forgives all your guilt,
who heals every one of your ills,
who redeems your life from the grave,
who crowns you with love and compassion.

3. The Lord does deeds of justice,
gives judgement for all who are oppressed.
He made known his ways to Moses
and his deeds to Israels's sons.

4. The Lord is compassion and love,
slow to anger and rich in mercy.
For as the heavens are high above the earth
so strong is his love for those who fear him.

SECOND READING   *1 Corinthians 10:1-6, 10-12*
The life of the people under Moses in the desert was written down to be a lesson for us.
I want to remind you, brothers, how our fathers were all guided by a cloud above them and how they all passed through the sea. They were all baptised into Moses in this cloud and in this sea; all ate the same spiritual food and all drank the same spiritual drink, since they all drank from the spiritual rock that followed them as they went, and that rock was Christ. In spite of this, most of them failed to please God and their corpses littered the desert.
These things all happened as warnings for us, not to have the wicked lusts for forbidden things that they had. You must never complain: some of them did, and they were killed by the Destroyer.
All this happened to them as a warning, and it was written down to be a lesson for us who are living at the end of the age. The man who thinks he is safe must be careful that he does not fall.
This is the word of the Lord. **Thanks be to God.**
All stand to greet the Gospel. If this Acclamation is not sung it may be omitted.
Repent, says the Lord, for the kingdom of heaven is close at hand.

THE GOSPEL   *Luke 13:1-9*
The Lord be with you. **And also with you**
A reading from the holy Gospel according to Luke. **Glory to you, Lord.**
Unless you repent you will all perish as they did.
It was about this time that some people arrived and told Jesus about the Galileans whose blood Pilate had mingled with that of their sacrifices. At this he said to them, "Do you suppose these Galileans who suffered like that were greater sinners than any other Galileans? They were not, I tell you. No; but unless you repent you will all perish as they did. Or those eighteen on whom the tower at Siloam fell and killed them? Do you suppose that they were more guilty than all the other people living in Jerusalem? They were not, I tell you. No; but unless you repent you will all perish as they did."
He told this parable: "A man had a fig tree planted in his vineyard, and he came looking for fruit on it but found none. He said to the man who looked after the vineyard, 'Look here, for three years now I have been coming to look for fruit on this fig tree and finding none. Cut it down: why should it be taking up the ground?' 'Sir,' the man replied 'leave it one more year and give me time to dig round it and manure it: it may bear fruit next year; if not, then you can cut it down.' "
This is the Gospel of the Lord. **Praise to you, Lord Jesus Christ.**
The Homily may follow, then Turn to page 6 for the Creed.

PRAYER OVER THE GIFTS
Lord,
by the grace of this sacrifice
may we who ask forgiveness
be ready to forgive one another.

Look favourably upon our sacrifice, Lord, and grant us this grace: that as we pray to be forgiven ourselves, we may be quick to forgive others.

Turn to page 12 for the Lent Prefaces

COMMUNION ANTIPHON

The sparrow even finds a home, the swallow finds a nest wherein to place her young, near to your altars, Lord of hosts, my King, my God! How happy they who dwell in your house! For ever they are praising you.

The sparrow has found herself a home, and the turtle-dove a nest for her young, by your altars, Lord of hosts, my King, my God.
They are happy who dwell in your house; they shall praise you for ever.

PRAYER AFTER COMMUNION

Lord,
in sharing this sacrament
may we receive your forgiveness
and be brought together in unity and
peace.

We have received, Lord, the pledge of what is in store for us in heaven; we have eaten our fill of the bread of life while still on earth. Grant that we may experience in our lives the effects of the sacrament we celebrate.

Turn to page 25 for the Concluding Rite

4th Sunday of Lent

As the priest goes to the altar everyone joins in the Entrance Antiphon or a hymn.

Rejoice, Jerusalem! Be glad for her, you who love her; rejoice with her, you who mourned for her, and you will find contentment at her consoling breasts.

Rejoice, Jerusalem, and rejoice with her all you who love her.
Rejoice and be cheerful, you who were desolate.
Be glad and take your fill of the milk of her consolation.

Turn to page 4

OPENING PRAYER

Father of peace,
we are joyful in your Word,
your Son Jesus Christ,
who reconciles us to you.
Let us hasten towards Easter
with the eagerness of faith and love.

O God, you have wonderfully reconciled the human race through Jesus Christ, your Word. Grant that your Christian people may prepare to celebrate the Paschal mystery with lively devotion and eager faith.

FIRST READING   *Joshua 5:9-12*

The People of God keep the Passover on their entry into the promised land.

The Lord said to Joshua, "Today I have taken the shame of Egypt away from you." The Israelites pitched their camp at Gilgal and kept the Passover there on the fourteenth day of the month, at evening in the plain of Jericho. On the morrow of the Passover they tasted the produce of that country, unleavened bread and roasted ears of corn, that same day. From that time, from their first eating of the produce of that country, the manna stopped falling. And having manna no longer, the Israelites fed from that year onwards on what the land of Canaan yielded.
This is the word of the Lord. **Thanks be to God.**

RESPONSORIAL PSALM   *Psalm 33*
Taste and see that the Lord is good.
1. I will bless the Lord at all times,   2. Glorify the Lord with me.
his praise always on my lips;   Together let us praise his name.
in the Lord my soul shall make its boast.   I sought the Lord and he answered me;
The humble shall hear and be glad.   from all my terrors he set me free.

3. Look towards him and be radiant;
let your faces not be abashed.
This poor man called; the Lord heard him
and rescued him from all his distress.

SECOND READING   *2 Corinthians 5:17-21*
God reconciled us to himself through Christ.

And for anyone who is in Christ, there is a new creation; the old creation has gone, and now the new one is here. It is all God's work. It was God who reconciled us to himself through Christ and gave us the work of handing on this reconciliation. In other words, God in Christ was reconciling the world to himself, not holding men's faults against them, and he has entrusted to us the news that they are reconciled. So we are ambassadors for Christ; it is as though God were appealing through us, and the appeal that we make in Christ's name is: be reconciled to God. For our sake God made the sinless one into sin, so that in him we might become the goodness of God. This is the word of the Lord. **Thanks be to God.**
All stand to greet the Gospel. If this Acclamation is not sung it may be omitted.
I will leave this place and go to my father and say: "Father, I have sinned against heaven and against you."

THE GOSPEL   *Luke 15:1-3, 11-32*
The Lord be with you. **And also with you.**
A reading from the holy Gospel according to Luke. **Glory to you, Lord.**
Your brother here was dead and has come to life.

The tax collectors and the sinners were all seeking the company of Jesus to hear what he had to say, and the Pharisees and the scribes complained. "This man" they said "welcomes sinners and eats with them." So he spoke this parable to them: "A man had two sons. The younger said to his father, 'Father, let me have the share of the estate that would come to me.' So the father divided the property between them. A few days later, the younger son got together everything he had and left for a distant country where he squandered his money on a life of debauchery.
"When he had spent it all, that country experienced a severe famine, and now he began to feel the pinch, so he hired himself out to one of the local inhabitants who put him on his farm to feed the pigs. And he would willingly have filled his belly with the husks the pigs were eating but no one offered him anything. Then he came to his senses and said, 'How many of my father's paid servants have more food than they want, and here am I dying of hunger! I will leave this place and go to my father and say: Father, I have sinned against heaven and against you; I no longer deserve to be called your son; treat me as one of your paid servants.' So he left the place and went back to his father.
"While he was still a long way off, his father saw him and was moved with pity. He ran to the boy, clasped him in his arms and kissed him tenderly. Then his son said, 'Father, I have sinned against heaven and against you. I no longer deserve to be

called your son.' But the father said to his servants, 'Quick! Bring out the best robe and put it on him; put a ring on his finger and sandals on his feet. Bring the calf we have been fattening, and kill it; we are going to have a feast, a celebration, because this son of mine was dead and has come back to life; he was lost and is found.' And they began to celebrate.

"Now the elder son was out in the fields, and on his way back, as he drew near the house, he could hear music and dancing. Calling one of the servants he asked what it was all about. 'Your brother has come' replied the servant 'and your father has killed the calf we had fattened because he has got him back safe and sound.' He was angry then and refused to go in, and his father came out to plead with him; but he answered his father, 'Look, all these years I have slaved for you and never once disobeyed your orders, yet you never offered me so much as a kid for me to celebrate with my friends. But, for this son of yours, when he comes back after swallowing up your property—he and his women—you kill the calf we had been fattening.'

"The father said. 'My son, you are with me always and all I have is yours. But it is only right we should celebrate and rejoice, because your brother here was dead and has come to life; he was lost and is found.' "

This is the Gospel of the Lord. **Praise to you, Lord Jesus Christ.**

The Homily may follow, then | *Turn to page 6 for the Creed.*

PRAYER OVER THE GIFTS

Lord,
we offer you these gifts
which bring us peace and joy.
Increase our reverence by this eucharist,
and bring salvation to the world.

Lord, it is with great joy that we offer you the sacrifice that brings everlasting healing. Grant us the grace to celebrate it for the world's salvation, with due reverence and obedience.

| *Turn to page 12 for the Lent Prefaces* |

COMMUNION ANTIPHON

**My son, you should
rejoice, because your
brother was dead and
has come back to life,
he was lost and is found.**

It is right, my son, for you to be glad, for your brother was dead and is alive again; he was lost and is found.

PRAYER AFTER COMMUNION

Father,
you enlighten all who come into the
world.
Fill our hearts with the light of your
gospel,
that our thoughts may please you,
and our love be sincere.

O God, you enlighten every man who comes into the world. Enlighten our hearts with the brightness of your grace, so that our thoughts may be worthy and pleasing to you, and our love for you may be constant and sincere.

| *Turn to page 25 for the Concluding Rite* |

5th Sunday of Lent

As the priest goes to the altar everyone joins in this Entrance Antiphon or a hymn.

Give me justice, O God, and defend my cause against the wicked; rescue me from deceitful and unjust men. You, O God, are my refuge.

Turn to page 4

Give judgment for me, O God, and defend my cause against a godless people; rescue me from wicked and deceitful men, for you are my God and my strength.

OPENING PRAYER

Father,
help us to be like Christ your Son,
who loved the world and died for our
　salvation.
Inspire us by his love,
guide us by his example,
who lives and reigns with you and the
　Holy Spirit,
one God, for ever and ever.

Lord, your Son in his love for the world gave himself up to death. Grant us the grace to live our lives in the same spirit of unhesitating love.

FIRST READING
Isaiah 43:16-21

See, I am doing a new deed, and I will give my chosen people drink.
Thus says the Lord, who made a way through the sea, a path in the great waters; who put chariots and horse in the field and a powerful army, which lay there never to rise again, snuffed out, put out like a wick: No need to recall the past, no need to think about what was done before. See, I am doing a new deed, even now it comes to light; can you not see it? Yes, I am making a road in the wilderness, paths in the wilds. The wild beasts will honour me, jackals and ostriches, because I am putting water in the wilderness (rivers in the wild) to give my chosen people drink. The people I have formed for myself will sing my praises.
This is the word of the Lord. **Thanks be to God.**

RESPONSORIAL PSALM
Psalm 125

What marvels the Lord worked for us! Indeed we were glad.

1. When the Lord delivered Zion from bondage,
it seemed like a dream.
Then was our mouth filled with laughter,
on our lips there were songs.
2. The heathens themsleves said: "What marvels the Lord worked for them!"
What marvels the Lord worked for us! Indeed we were glad.

3. Deliver us, O Lord, from our bondage
as streams in dry land.
Those who are sowing in tears
will sing when they reap.
4. They go out, they go out, full of tears, carrying seed for the sowing:
they come back, they come back, full of song,
carrying their sheaves.

SECOND READING
Philippians 3:8-14

Reproducing the pattern of his death, I have accepted the loss of everything for Christ.
I believe nothing can happen that will outweigh the supreme advantage of knowing

Christ Jesus my Lord. For him I have accepted the loss of everything, and I look on everything as so much rubbish if only I can have Christ and be given a place in him. I am no longer trying for perfection by my own efforts, the perfection that comes from the Law, but I want only the perfection that comes through faith in Christ, and is from God and based on faith. All I want is to know Christ and the power of his resurrection and to share his sufferings by reproducing the pattern of his death. That is the way I can hope to take my place in the resurrection of the dead. Not that I have become perfect yet: I have not yet won, but I am still running, trying to capture the prize for which Christ Jesus captured me. I can assure you my brothers, I am far from thinking that I have already won. All I can say is that I forget the past and I strain ahead for what is still to come; I am racing for the finish, for the prize to which God calls us upwards to receive in Christ Jesus.

This is the word of the Lord. **Thanks be to God.**

All stand to greet the Gospel. If this Acclamation is not sung it may be omitted.
Seek good and not evil so that you may live, and that the Lord God of hosts may really be with you.

THE GOSPEL *John 8:1-11*

The Lord be with you. **And also with you.**

A reading from the holy Gospel according to John. **Glory to you Lord.**

If there is one of you who has not sinned, let him be the first to throw a stone at her.

Jesus went to the Mount of Olives. At daybreak he appeared in the Temple again; and as all the people came to him, he sat down and began to teach them.

The scribes and Pharisees brought a woman along who had been caught committing adultery; and making her stand there in full view of everybody, they said to Jesus, "Master, this woman was caught in the very act of committing adultery, and Moses has ordered us in the Law to condemn women like this to death by stoning. What have you to say?" They asked him this as a test, looking for something to use against him. But Jesus bent down and started writing on the ground with his finger. As they persisted with their question, he looked up and said, "If there is one of you who has not sinned, let him be the first to throw a stone at her." Then he bent down and wrote on the ground again. When they heard this they went away one by one, beginning with the eldest, until Jesus was left alone with the woman, who remained standing there. He looked up and said, "Woman, where are they? Has no one condemned you?" "No one, sir", she replied. "Neither do I condemn you," said Jesus "go away, and don't sin any more."

This is the Gospel of the Lord. **Praise to you, Lord Jesus Christ.**

The Homily may follow, then Turn to page 6 for the Creed.

PRAYER OVER THE GIFTS

Almighty God,
may the sacrifice we offer
take away the sins of those
whom you enlighten with the Christian faith.

Almighty God, you have given us the teachings of the Christian faith to enlighten our minds. Grant that the grace of this sacrifice may purify our hearts.

Turn to page 12 for the Lent Prefaces

COMMUNION ANTIPHON

Has no one condemned you? The woman answered: No one, Lord. Neither do I condemn you: go and do not sin again.

Woman, has no one condemned you? No one, Lord. Neither do I condemn you; do not sin again.

PRAYER AFTER COMMUNION

Almighty Father, by this sacrifice may we always remain one with your Son, Jesus Christ, whose body and blood we share, for he is Lord for ever and ever.

Almighty God, we have received your Son's body and blood. Grant us the grace always to be numbered among his members: who lives and reigns for ever and ever.

Turn to page 25 for the Concluding Rite

Passion Sunday

COMMEMORATION OF THE LORD'S ENTRANCE INTO JERUSALEM

First Form: The Procession

The people assemble, holding palm branches. This antiphon or another is sung:

Hosanna to the Son of David, *Matthew 21:9*
the King of Israel.
Blessed is he who comes
in the name of the Lord.
Hosanna in the highest.

The priest greets the people in these or similar words:

Dear friends in Christ, for five weeks of Lent we have been preparing, by works of charity and self-sacrifice, for the celebration of our Lord's paschal mystery. Today we come together to begin this solemn celebration in union with the whole Church throughout the world. Christ entered in triumph into his own city, to complete his work as our Messiah: to suffer, to die, and to rise again. Let us remember with devotion this entry which began his saving work and follow him with a lively faith. United with him in his suffering on the cross, may we share his resurrection and new life.

The priest says one of the following prayers:

Almighty God, we pray you bless + these branches and make them holy. Today we joyfully acclaim Jesus our Messiah and King. May we reach one day the happiness of the new and everlasting Jerusalem by faithfully following him who lives and reigns for ever and ever. **Amen.**

Lord, increase the faith of your people and listen to our prayers. Today we honour Christ our triumphant King by carrying these branches. May we honour you every day by living always in him, for he is Lord for ever and ever. **Amen.**

The priest sprinkles the branches with holy water.

Luke 19:28-40

The Lord be with you. **And also with you.**
A reading from the holy Gospel according to Luke. **Glory to you, Lord.**

Blessings on him who comes in the name of the Lord.

Jesus went on ahead, going up to Jerusalem. Now when he was near Bethphage and Bethany, close by the Mount of Olives as it is called, he sent two of the disciples, telling them, "Go off to the village opposite, and as you enter it you will find a tethered colt that no one has yet ridden. Untie it and bring it here. If anyone asks you, 'Why are you untying it?' you are to say this, 'The Master needs it.' " The messengers went off and found everything just as he had told them. As they were untying the colt, its owner said, "Why are you untying that colt?" and they answered, "The Master needs it."

So they took the colt to Jesus, and throwing their garments over its back they helped Jesus on to it. As he moved off, people spread their cloaks in the road, and now, as he was approaching the downward slope of the Mount of Olives, the whole group of disciples joyfully began to praise God at the top of their voices for all the miracles they had seen. They cried out: "Blessings on the King who comes, in the name of the Lord! Peace in heaven and glory in the highest heavens!"

Some Pharisees in the crowd said to him, "Master, check your disciples," but he answered, "I tell you, if these keep silence the stones will cry out."

This is the Gospel of the Lord. **Praise to you, Lord Jesus Christ.**

A short homily may now be given. Before the procession begins the priest may address the people in these or similar words:

Let us go forth in peace,
praising Jesus our Messiah,
as did the crowds who welcomed him to Jerusalem.

The procession to the church begins. During the procession, this hymn may be sung:

All glory, laud and honour,
To thee, Redeemer King,
To whom the lips of children
Made sweet hosannas ring.

1. Thou are the King of Israel,
   Thou David's royal Son,
   Who in the Lord's name comest,
   The King and blessed one.

2. The company of angels
   Are praising thee on high,
   And mortal men and all things
   Created make reply.

3. The people of the Hebrews
   With palms before thee went:
   Our praise and prayer and anthems
   Before thee we present.

4. To thee before thy passion
   They sang their hymns of praise;
   To thee now high exalted
   Our melody we raise.

5. Thou didst accept their praises,
   Accept the prayers we bring,
   Who in all good delightest,
   Thou good and gracious King.

The Mass now begins with the Opening Prayer (see next page).

Second Form: The Solemn entrance

If the procession cannot be held outside the church, the commemoration of the Lord's entrance into Jerusalem takes place inside.

The people assemble, holding palm branches, while the priest and ministers, with a representative group of the faithful, go to a suitable place in the church outside the

sanctuary, so that most of the people will be able to see.
The antiphon 'Hosanna' (see Page 83) or another suitable song is sung. Then the
branches are blessed (page 83), and the Gospel proclaimed (page 84). After the
Gospel the priest, ministers and faithful move solemnly through the church to the
sanctuary while 'All Glory, Laud and Honour', or a similar song is sung. The Mass
then begins with the Opening Prayer (see below).

Third Form: The Simple Entrance
As the priest goes to the altar everyone joins in this Entrance Antiphon or a hymn.
**Six days before the solemn passover the Lord came to Jerusalem, and children waving
palm branches ran out to welcome him. They loudly praised the Lord: Hosanna in the
highest. Blessed are you who have come to us so rich in love and mercy.**

1. Open wide the doors and gates.
Lift high the ancient portals.
The King of glory enters.

2. Who is this King of glory?
He is God the mighty Lord.

3. Hosanna in the highest.
**Blessed are you who have come to us
so rich in love and mercy.**

Turn to page 4

OPENING PRAYER
Almighty, ever-living God,
you have given the human race Jesus Christ our Saviour
as a model of humility.
He fulfilled your will
by becoming man and giving his life on the cross.
Help us to bear witness to you
by following his example of suffering
and make us worthy to share in his resurrection.

FIRST READING   *Isaiah 50:4-7*
I did not cover my face against insult, I know I shall not be shamed.
The Lord has given me a disciple's tongue. So that I may know how to reply to the
wearied he provides me with speech. Each morning he wakes me to hear, to listen
like a disciple. The Lord has opened my ear.
For my part, I made no resistance, neither did I turn away. I offered my back to
those who struck me, my cheeks to those who tore at my beard; I did not cover my
face against insult and spittle.
The Lord comes to my help, so that I am untouched by the insults. So, too, I set my
face like flint; I know I shall not be shamed.
This is the word of the Lord. **Thanks be to God.**

RESPONSORIAL PSALM
My God, my God, why have you forsaken me?   *Ps. 21:8-9, 17-20, 23-24. R.v.2*

1. All who see me deride me.
They curl their lips, they toss their
   heads.
'He trusted in the Lord, let him save
   him;
let him release him if this is his friend.'

2. Many dogs have surrounded me,
a band of the wicked beset me,
They tear holes in my hands and my feet
I can count every one of my bones.

3. They divide my clothing among them.
They cast lots for my robe.
O Lord, do not leave me alone,
my strength, make hast to help me!

4. I will tell of your name to my brethen and praise you where they are assembled.
'You who fear the Lord give him praise; all sons of Jacob, give him glory. Revere him, Israel's sons.'

SECOND READING
Philippians 2:6-11

He humbled himself, but God raised him high.

His state was divine, yet Christ Jesus did not cling to his equality with God but emptied himself to assume the condition of a slave, and became as men are; and being as all men are, he was humbler yet, even to accepting death, death on a cross. But God raised him high and gave him the name which is above all other names so that all beings in the heavens, on earth and in the underworld, should bend the knee at the name of Jesus and that every tongue should acclaim Jesus Christ as Lord, to the glory of God the Father.
This is the word of the Lord. **Thanks be to God.**

All stand to greet the Gospel. If this Acclamation is not sung it may omitted.
Christ was humbler yet, even to accepting death, death on a cross. But God raised him high and gave him the name which is above all names.

THE PASSION
Luke 22:14-23:56

The passion of our Lord Jesus Christ according to Luke. **Glory to you, Lord.**

When the hour came Jesus took his place at table, and the apostles with him. And he said to them, 'I have longed to eat this passover with you before I suffer; because, I tell you, I shall not eat it again until it is fulfilled in the kingdom of God.'
Then, taking a cup, he gave thanks and said, 'Take this and share it among you, because from now on, I tell you, I shall not drink wine until the kingdom of God comes.'
Then he took some bread, and when he had given thanks, broke it and gave it to them, saying, 'This is my body which will be given for you; do this as a memorial of me.' He did the same with the cup after supper, and said, 'This cup is the new covenant in my blood which will be poured out for you.
'And yet, here with me on the table is the hand of the man who betrays me. The Son of Man does indeed go to his fate even as it has been decreed, but alas for that man by whom he is betrayed!' And they began to ask one another which of them it could be who was to do this thing.
A dispute arose also between them about which should be reckoned the greatest, but he said to them, 'Among pagans it is the kings who lord it over them, and those who have authority over them are given title Benefactor. This must not happen with you. No; the greatest among you must behave as if he were the youngest, the leader as if he were the one who serves. For who is the greater: the one at table or the one who serves? The one at table, surely? Yet here am I among you as one who serves!
'You are the men who have stood by me faithfully in my trials; and now I confer a kingdom on you, just as my Father conferred one on me: you will eat and drink at my table in my kingdom, and you will sit on thrones to judge the twelve tribes of Israel.
'Simon, Simon! Satan, you must know, has got his wish to sift you all like wheat;

but I have prayed for you, Simon, that your faith may not fail, and once you have recovered, you in your turn must strengthen your brothers.' 'Lord,' he answered, 'I would be ready to go to prison with you, and to death.' Jesus replied, 'I tell you, Peter by the time the cock crows today you will have denied three times that you know me.'

He said to them, 'When I sent you out without purse or haversack or sandals, were you short of anything?' 'No' they said. He said to them, 'But now if you have a purse, take it; if you have a haversack, do the same; if you have no sword, sell your cloak and buy one, because I tell you these words of scripture have to be fulfilled in me: He let himself be taken for a criminal. Yes, what scripture says about me is even now reaching its fulfilment.' They said **'Lord, there are two swords here now.'** He said to them, 'That is enough!' He then left the upper room to make his way as usual to the Mount of Olives, with the disciples following. When they reached the place he said to them, 'Pray not to be put to the test.'

Then he withdrew from them, about a stone's throw away, and knelt down and prayed. 'Father,' he said, 'if you are willing, take this cup away from me. Nevertheless, let your will be done, not mine.' Then an angel appeared to him, coming from heaven to give him strength. In his anguish he prayed even more earnestly, and his sweat fell to the ground like great drops of blood.

When he rose from prayer he went to the disciples and found them sleeping for sheer grief. 'Why are you asleep?' he said to them. 'Get up and pray not to be put to the test.' He was still speaking when a number of men appeared, and at the head of them the man called Judas, one of the Twelve, who went up to Jesus to kiss him. Jesus said, 'Judas, are you betraying the Son of Man with a kiss?' His followers, seeing what was happening, said, **'Lord, shall we use our swords?'** And one of them struck out at the high priest's servant, and cut off his right ear. But at this Jesus spoke. 'Leave off!' he said 'That will do!' And touching the man's ear he healed him.

Then Jesus spoke to the chief priests and captains of the Temple guard and elders who had come for him. 'Am I a brigand' he said 'that you had to set out with swords and clubs? When I was among you in the Temple day after day you never moved to lay hands on me. But this is your hour; this is the reign of darkness.'

They seized him then and led him away, and they took him to the high priest's house. Peter followed at a distance. They had lit a fire in the middle of the courtyard and Peter sat down among them and as he was sitting there by the blaze a servant-girl saw him, peered at him, and said, 'This person was with him too.' But he denied it. 'Woman,' he said 'I do not know him.' Shortly afterwards someone else saw him and said, 'You are another of them.' But Peter replied, 'I am not, my friend.' About an hour later another man insisted saying, 'This fellow was certainly with him. Why, he is a Galilean.' 'My friend,' said Peter 'I do not know what you are talking about.' At that instant, while he was still speaking, the cock crew, and the Lord turned and looked straight at Peter, and Peter remembered what the Lord had said to him, 'Before the cock crows today, you will have disowned me three times.' And he went outside and wept bitterly.

Meanwhile the men who guarded Jesus were mocking and beating him. They blindfolded him and questioned him, they said, **'Play the prophet. Who hit you then?'** And they continued heaping insults on him.

When day broke there was a meeting of the elders of the people, attended by the chief priests and scribes. He was brought before their council, and they said to him, **'If you are the Christ, tell us.'** 'If I tell you,' he replied 'you will not believe me, and if I question you, you will not answer. But from now on, the Son of Man will be seated at the right hand of the Power of God.' Then they all said, **'So you are the Son of God then?** He answered, 'It is you who say I am.' **'What need of witnesses have we now? We have heard it for ourselves from his own lips.'** The whole assembly then rose, and they brought him before Pilate.

They began their accusation by saying, **'We found this man inciting our people to revolt, opposing payment of tribute to Caesar, and claiming to be Christ, a king.'** Pilate put to him this question, 'Are you the king of the Jews?' 'It is you who say it' he replied. Pilate then said to the chief priests and the crowd, 'I find no case against this man.' But they persisted, **'He is inflaming the people with his teaching all over Judaea; it has come all the way from Galilee, where he started, down to here.'** When Pilate heard this, he asked if the man were a Galilean; and finding that he came under Herod's jurisdiction he passed him over to Herod who was in Jerusalem at that time. Herod was delighted to see Jesus; he had heard about him and had been wanting for a long time to set eyes on him; moreover, he was hoping to see some miracle worked by him. So he questioned him at some length; but without getting any reply. Meanwhile the chief priests and the scribes were there, violently pressing their accusations. Then Herod, together with his guards, treated him with contempt and made fun of him; he put a rich cloak on him and sent him back to Pilate. And though Herod and Pilate had been enemies before, they were reconciled that same day.

Pilate then summoned the chief priests and the leading men and the people. 'You brought this man before me' he said 'as a political agitator. Now I have gone into the matter myself in your presence and found no case against the man in respect of all the charges you bring against him. Nor has Herod either, since he has sent him back to us. As you can see, the man has done nothing that deserves death, so I shall have him flogged and then let him go.' But as one man they howled, **'Away with him! Give us Barabbas!'** (This man had been thrown into prison for causing a riot in the city and for murder.)

Pilate was anxious to set Jesus free and addressed them again, but they shouted back, **'Crucify him! Crucify him!'** And for the third time he spoke to them, 'Why? What harm has this man done? I have found no case against him that deserves death, so I shall have him punished and then let him go.' But they kept on shouting at the top of their voices, demanding that he should be crucified. And their shouts were growing louder.

Pilate then gave his verdict: their demand was to be granted. He released the man they asked for, who had been imprisoned for rioting and murder, and handed Jesus over to them to deal with as they pleased.

As they were leading him away they seized on a man, Simon from Cyrene, who was coming in from the country, and made him shoulder the cross and carry it behind Jesus. Large numbers of people followed him, and of women too, who mourned and lamented for him. But Jesus turned to them and said, 'Daughters of Jerusalem, do not weep for me; weep rather for yourselves and for your children. For the days will surely come when people will say, "Happy are those who are barren, the wombs that have never borne, the breasts that have never suckled!" Then they will begin to say to the mountains, 'Fall on us!"'; to the hills, "Cover us!" For if men use the green wood like this, what will happen when it is dry?" Now with him they were also leading out two other criminals to be executed.

When they reached the place called The Skull, they crucified him there and the two criminals also, one on the right, the other on the left. Jesus said, 'Father, forgive them; they do not know what they are doing.' Then they cast lots to share out his clothing.

The people stayed there watching him. As for the leaders, they jeered at him **'He saved others, let him save himself if he is the Christ of God, the Chosen One.'** The soldiers mocked him too, and when they approached to offer him vinegar they said, **'If you are the king of the Jews, save yourself.'** Above him there was an inscription: 'This is the King of the Jews.'

One of the criminals hanging there abused him. 'Are you not the Christ?' he said. 'Save yourself and us as well.' But the other spoke up and rebuked him. 'Have you no fear of God at all?' he said. 'You got the same sentence as he did, but in our case we deserved it: we are paying for what we did. But this man has done nothing wrong. Jesus,' he said 'remember me when you come into your kingdom.' 'Indeed, I promise you,' he replied 'today you will be with me in paradise.'

It was now about the sixth hour and with the sun eclipsed, a darkness came over the whole land until the ninth hour. The veil of the Temple was torn right down the middle; and when Jesus had cried out in a loud voice, he said, 'Father, into your hands I commit my spirit.' With these words he breathed his last.

When the centurion saw what had taken place, he gave praise to God and said, 'This was a great and good man.' And when all the people who had gathered for the spectacle saw what had happened, they went home beating their breasts.

All his friends stood at a distance; so also did the women who had accompanied him from Galilee, and they saw all this happen.

Then a member of the council arrived, an upright and virtuous man named Joseph. He had not consented to what the others had planned and carried out. He came from Arimathaea, a Jewish town, and he lived in the hope of seeing the kingdom of God. This man went to Pilate and asked for the body of Jesus. He then took it down, wrapped it in a shroud and put him in a tomb which was hewn in stone in which no one had yet been laid. It was Preparation Day and the sabbath was imminent.

Meanwhile the women who had come from Galilee with Jesus were following behind. They took note of the tomb and of the position of the body.

Then they returned and prepared spices and ointments. And on the sabbath day they rested, as the Law required.

The Homily may follow, then Turn to page 6 for the Creed.

PRAYER OVER THE GIFTS
Lord,
may the suffering and death of Jesus, your only Son,
make us pleasing to you.
Alone we can do nothing,
but may this perfect sacrifice
win us your mercy and love.

Turn to page 13 for the Preface of Passion Sunday

COMMUNION ANTIPHON
Father, if this cup may not pass, but I must drink it, then your will be done.

PRAYER AFTER COMMUNION
Lord,
you have satisfied our hunger with this eucharistic food.
The death of your Son gives us hope and strengthens our faith.
May his resurrection give us perseverance
and lead us to salvation.

Turn to page 25 for the Concluding Rite

EVENING MASS OF THE LORD'S SUPPER

Holy Thursday

As the priest goes to the altar everyone joins in this Entrance Antiphon or a hymn.
We should glory in the cross of our Lord Jesus Christ, for he is our salvation, our life and our resurrection; through him we are saved and made free.

Turn to page 4

OPENING PRAYER
God our Father,
we are gathered here to share in the supper
which your only Son left to his Church to reveal his love.
He gave it to us when he was about to die
and commanded us to celebrate it as the new and eternal sacrifice.
We pray that in this eucharist
we may find the fullness of love and life.

FIRST READING   *Exodus 12:1-8, 11-14*

Instructions concerning the Passover meal.

The Lord said to Moses and Aaron in the land of Egypt, 'This month is to be the first of all the others for you, the first month of your year. Speak to the whole community of Israel and say, "On the tenth day of this month each man must take an animal from the flock, one for each family: one animal for each household. If the household is too small to eat the animal, a man must join with his neighbour, the nearest to his house, as the number of persons requires. You must take into account what each can eat in deciding the number for the animal. It must be an animal without blemish, a male one year old; you may take it from either sheep or goats. You must keep it till the fourteenth day of the month when the whole assembly of the community of Israel shall slaughter it between the two evenings. Some of the blood must then be taken and put on the two doorposts and the lintel of the houses where it is eaten. That night, the flesh is to be eaten, roasted over the fire; it must be eaten with unleavened bread and bitter herbs. You shall eat it like this: with a girdle round your waist, sandals on your feet, a staff in your hand. You shall eat it hastily: it is a passover in honour of the Lord. That night, I will go through the land of Egypt and

strike down all the first-born in the land of Egypt, man and beast alike, and I shall deal out punishment to all the gods of Egypt, I am the Lord. The blood shall serve to mark the houses that you live in. When I see the blood I will pass over you and you shall escape the destroying plague when I strike the land of Egypt. This day is to be a day of remembrance for you, and you must celebrate it as a feast in the Lord's honour. For all generations you are to declare it a day of festival, for ever." '
This is the word of the Lord. **Thanks be to God.**

RESPONSORIAL PSALM   *Ps 115:12-13, 15-18.R1 Cor 10:16*
The blessing-cup that we bless is a communion with the blood of Christ.

1. How can I repay the Lord   2. O precious in the eyes of the Lord
for his goodness to me?   is the death of his faithful.
The cup of salvation I will raise;   Your servant, Lord, your servant am I;
I will call on the Lord's name.   you have loosened my bonds.

3. A thanksgiving sacrifice I make;
I will call on the Lord's name.
My vows to the Lord I will fulfil
before all his people.

SECOND READING   *Corinthians 11:23-26*
Every time you eat this bread and drink this cup, you are proclaiming the death of the Lord.
For this is what I received from the Lord, and in turn passed on to you; that on the same night that he was betrayed, the Lord Jesus took some bread, and thanked God for it and broke it, and he said, 'This is my body, which is for you; do this as a memorial of me.' In the same way he took the cup after supper, and said, 'This cup is the new covenant in my blood. Whenever you drink it, do this as a memorial of me.' Until the Lord comes, therefore, every time you eat this bread and drink this cup, you are proclaiming his death.
This is the word of the Lord. **Thanks be to God.**
All stand to greet the Gospel. If this Acclamation is not sung it may be omitted.
I give you a new commandment: love one another just as I have loved you, says the Lord.

THE GOSPEL   *John 13:1-15*
The Lord be with you. **And also with you.**
A reading from the holy Gospel according to John. **Glory to you, Lord.**
Now he showed how perfect his love was.
It was before the festival of the Passover, and Jesus knew that the hour had come for him to pass from this world to the Father. He had always loved those who were his in the world, but now he showed how perfect his love was.
They were at supper, and the devil had already put it into the mind of Judas Iscariot son of Simon, to betray him. Jesus knew that the Father had put everything into his hands, and that he had come from God and was returning to God, and he got up from the table, removed his outer garment and, taking a towel, wrapped it round his waist; he then poured water into a basin and began to wash the disciples' feet and to wipe them with the towel he was wearing.
He came to Simon Peter, who said to him, 'Lord, are you going to wash my feet?'
Jesus answered, 'At the moment you do not know what I am doing, but later you

will understand.' 'Never!' said Peter 'You shall never wash my feet.' Jesus replied, 'If I do not wash you, you can have nothing in common with me.' 'Then, Lord,' said Simon Peter 'not only my feet, but my hands and my head as well!' Jesus said, 'No one who has taken a bath needs washing, he is clean all over. You too are clean, though not all of you are.' He knew who was going to betray him, that was why he said, 'though not all of you are.'

When he had washed their feet and put on his clothes again he went back to the table. 'Do you understand' he said 'what I have done to you? You call me Master and Lord, and rightly; so I am. If I, then, the Lord and Master, have washed your feet, you should wash each other's feet. I have given you an example so that you may copy what I have done to you.'

This is the Gospel of the Lord. **Praise to you, Lord Jesus Christ.**

WASHING OF FEET

This ceremony may follow the homily according to custom. While the priest washes the feet of twelve men the following antiphons or similar songs are sung:

Antiphon 1   *see Jn. 13:4,5,15*
The Lord Jesus,
when he had eaten with his disciples,
poured water into a basin
and began to wash their feet, saying:
This example I leave you.

Antiphon 2   *Jn. 13:6,7,8*
Lord, do you wash my feet?
Jesus said to him:
If I do not wash your feet,
you can have no part with me.
℣ So he came to Simon Peter,
who said to him:
Lord, do you wash my feet?
℣ Now you do not know what I am doing,
but later you will understand.
Lord, do you wash my feet?

Antiphon 3   *See Jn. 13:14*
If I, your Lord and Teacher, have
   washed your feet,
then surely you must wash one another's
   feet.

Antiphon 4   *Jn 13:35*
If there is this love among you,
all will know that you are my disciples.
℣ Jesus said to his disciples:
If there is this love among you,
all will know that you are my disciples.

Antiphon 5   *Jn. 13:34*
I give you a new commandment:
love one another as I have loved you,
   says the Lord.

Antiphon 6   *1 Cor. 13:13*
Faith, hope, and love,
let these endure among you;
and the greatest of these is love.

Turn to page 7 for the Offertory Prayers

PRAYERS OVER THE GIFTS
Lord,
make us worthy to celebrate these mysteries.
Each time we offer this memorial sacrifice
the work of our redemption is accomplished.

Turn to page 13 for the Preface of Holy Thursday

COMMUNION ANTIPHON
This body will be given for you. This is the cup of the new convenant in my blood; whenever you receive them, do so in remembrance of me.

PRAYER AFTER COMMUNION
Almighty God,
we receive new life
from the supper your Son gave us in this world.
May we find full contentment
in the meal we hope to share
in your eternal kingdom.

TRANSFER OF THE HOLY EUCHARIST
*The Blessed Sacrament is now taken in procession to the Altar of Repose where it will
remain until tomorrow. A suitable Eucharistic hymn, such as 'Pange lingua' is sung.
After a period of silent adoration the priest returns to the sacristy.*

CELEBRATION OF THE LORD'S PASSION

Good Friday

*The priest and ministers go to the altar. They genuflect and prostrate themselves, or
they may kneel. All pray silently for a while. Then the priest says one of the following
prayers:*

Lord,
by shedding his blood for us,
your Son, Jesus Christ,
established the paschal mystery.
In your goodness, make us holy
and watch over us always.

Lord,
by the suffering of Christ your Son
you have saved us all from the death
we inherited from sinful Adam.
By the law of nature
we have borne the likeness of his
manhood.
May the sanctifying power of grace
help us to put on the likeness of our
Lord in heaven,
who lives and reigns for ever and ever.

FIRST PART: LITURGY OF THE WORD
FIRST READING *Isaiah 52:13-53:12*
He was pierced through for our faults.
See, my servant will prosper, he shall be lifted up, exalted, rise to great heights.
As the crowds were appalled on seeing him—so disfigured did he look that he
seemed no longer human—so will the crowds be astonished at him, and kings stand
speechless before him; for they shall see something never told and witness
something never heard before: 'Who could believe what we have heard, and to
whom has the power of the Lord been revealed?'
Like a sapling he grew up in front of us, like a root in arid ground. Without beauty,
without majesty (we saw him), no looks to attract our eyes; a thing despised and
rejected by men, a man of sorrows and familiar with suffering, a man to make people
screen their faces; he was despised and we took no account of him. And yet ours
were the sufferings he bore, ours the sorrows he carried. But we, we thought of him
as someone punished, struck by God, and brought low. Yet he was pierced through

for our faults, crushed for our sins. On him lies a punishment that brings us peace, and through his wounds we are healed. We had all gone astray like sheep, each taking his own way, and the Lord burdened him with the sins of all of us. Harshly dealt with, he bore it humbly, he never opened his mouth, like a lamb that is led to the slaughterhouse, like a sheep that is dumb before its shearers never opening its mouth.

By force and by law he was taken; would anyone plead his cause? Yes, he was torn away from the land of the living; for our faults struck down in death. They gave him a grave with the wicked, a tomb with the rich, though he had done no wrong and there had been no perjury in his mouth. The Lord has been pleased to crush him with suffering. If he offers his life in atonement, he shall see his heirs, he shall have a long life and through him what the Lord wishes will be done.

His soul's anguish over he shall see the light and be content. By his sufferings shall my servant justify many, taking their faults on himself.

Hence I will grant whole hordes for his tribute, he shall divide the spoil with the mighty, for surrendering himself to death and letting himself be taken for a sinner, while he was bearing the faults of many and praying all the time for sinners. This is the word of the Lord. **Thanks be to God.**

RESPONSORIAL PSALM　　　　　　　　*Ps 30:2, 6, 12-13, 15-17, 25.R.Lk 23:46*

Father, into your hands I commend my spirit.

1. In you, O Lord, I take refuge.
Let me never be put to shame.
In your justice, set me free.
Into your hands I commend my spirit.
It is you who will redeem me, Lord.

2. In the face of all my foes
I am a reproach,
an object of scorn to my neighbours
and of fear to my friends.

3. Those who see me in the street
run far away from me.
I am like a dead man, forgotten in
　men's hearts,
like a thing thrown away.

4. But as for me, I trust in you, Lord,
I say: 'You are my God.'
My life is in your hands, deliver me
from the hands of those who hate me.

5. Let your face shine on your servant.
Save me in your love.
Be strong, let your heart take courage,
all who hope in the Lord.

SECOND READING　　　　　　　　　　*Hebrews 4:14-16;5;7-9*

He learnt to obey through suffering and became for all who obey him the source of eternal salvation.

Since in Jesus, the Son of God, we have the supreme high priest who has gone through to the highest heaven, we must never let go of the faith that we have professed. For it is not as if we had a high priest who was incapable of feeling our weaknesses with us; but we have one who has been tempted in every way that we are, though he is without sin. Let us be confident, then, in approaching the throne of grace, that we shall have mercy from him and find grace when we are in need of help. During his life on earth, he offered up prayer and entreaty, aloud and in silent tears, to the one who had the power to save him out of death, and he submitted so humbly that his prayer was heard. Although he was a Son, he learnt to obey through suffering; but having been made perfect, he became for all who obey him the source of eternal salvation.

This is the word of the Lord. **Thanks be to God.**
All stand to greet the Gospel. If this Acclamation is not sung it may be omitted.
Christ was humbler yet, even to accepting death, death on a cross. But God raised him high and gave him the name which is above all names.

THE GOSPEL   *John 18:1-19:42*
The Passion of our Lord Jesus Christ according to John. **Glory to you, Lord.**

Jesus left with his disciples and crossed the Kedron valley. There was a garden there, and he went into it with his disciples. Judas the traitor knew the place well, since Jesus had often met his disciples there, and he brought the cohort to this place together with a detachment of guards sent by the chief priests and the Pharisees, all with lanterns and torches and weapons. Knowing everything that was going to happen to him, Jesus then came forward and said, 'Who are you looking for?' They answered, **'Jesus the Nazarene.'** He said, 'I am he.' Now Judas the traitor was standing among them. When Jesus said, 'I am he', they moved back and fell to the ground. He asked them a second time, 'Who are you looking for?' They said, **'Jesus the Nazarene.'** 'I have told you that I am he' replied Jesus. 'If I am the one you are looking for, let these others go.' This was to fulfil the words he had spoken, 'Not one of those you gave me have I lost.'
Simon Peter, who carried a sword, drew it and wounded the high priest's servant, cutting off his right ear. The servant's name was Malchus. Jesus said to Peter, 'Put your sword back in its scabbard; am I not to drink the cup that the Father has given me?'
The cohort and its captain and the Jewish guards seized Jesus and bound him. They took him first to Annas, because Annas was the father-in-law of Caiaphas, who was high priest that year. It was Caiaphas who had suggested to the Jews, 'It is better for one man to die for the people.'
Simon Peter, with another disciple, followed Jesus. This disciple, who was known to the high priest, went with Jesus into the high priest's palace, but Peter stayed outside the door. So the other disciple, the one known to the high priest, went out, spoke to the woman who was keeping the door and brought Peter in. The maid on duty at the door said to Peter, 'Aren't you another of that man's disciples?' He answered, 'I am not.' Now it was cold, and the servants and guards had lit a charcoal fire and were standing there warming themselves; so Peter stood there too, warming himself with the others.
The high priest questioned Jesus about his disciples and his teaching. Jesus answered, 'I have spoken openly for all the world to hear; I have always taught in the synagogue and in the Temple where all the Jews meet together: I have said nothing in secret. But why ask me? Ask my hearers what I taught; they know what I said.' At these words, one of the guards standing by gave Jesus a slap in the face saying, 'Is that the way to answer the high priest?' Jesus replied, 'If there is something wrong in what I said, point it out; but if there is no offence in it, why do you strike me?' Then Annas sent him, still bound, to Caiaphas the high priest.
As Simon Peter stood there warming himself, someone said to him, 'Aren't you another of his disciples? He denied it saying, 'I am not.' One of the high priest's servants, a relation of the man whose ear Peter had cut off, said, 'Didn't I see you in the garden with him?' Again Peter denied it; and at once a cock crew.
They then led Jesus from the house of Caiaphas to the Praetorium. It was now

morning. They did not go into the Praetorium themselves or they would be defiled and unable to eat the passover. So Pilate came outside to them and said, 'What charge do you bring against this man?' They replied, **'If he were not a criminal, we should not be handing him over to you.'** Pilate said, 'Take him yourselves, and try him by your own Law.' The Jews answered, **'We are not allowed to put a man to death.'** This was to fulfil the words Jesus had spoken indicating the way he was going to die. So Pilate went back into the Praetorium and called Jesus to him, 'Are you the king of the Jews?' he asked. Jesus replied, 'Do you ask this of your own accord, or have others spoken to you about me?' Pilate answered, 'Am I a Jew? It is your own people and the chief priests who have handed you over to me: what have you done?' Jesus replied, 'Mine is not a kingdom of this world; if my kingdom were of this world, my men would have fought to prevent my being surrendered to the Jews. But my kingdom is not of this kind.' 'So you are a king then?' said Pilate. 'It is you who say it' answered Jesus. 'Yes, I am a king. I was born for this, I came into the world for this; to bear witness to the truth; and all who are on the side of truth listen to my voice.' 'Truth?' said Pilate 'What is that?'; and with that he went out again to the Jews and said, 'I find no case against him. But according to a custom of yours I should release one prisoner at the Passover; would you like me, then, to release the king of the Jews?' At this they shouted: **'Not this man, but Barrabas.'** Barabbas was a brigand.

Pilate then had Jesus taken away and scourged; and after this, the soldiers twisted some thorns into a crown and put it on his head, and dressed him in a purple robe. They kept coming up to him and saying, **'Hail, king of the Jews!'** and they slapped him in the face.

Pilate came outside again and said to them, 'Look, I am going to bring him out to you to let you see that I find no case.' Jesus then came out wearing the crown of thorns and the purple robe. Pilate said, 'Here is the man.' When they saw him the chief priests and the guards shouted, **'Crucify him! Crucify him!'** Pilate said, 'Take him yourselves and crucify him: I can find no case against him.' The Jews replied **'We have a Law, and according to the Law he ought to die, because he claimed to be the Son of God.'**

When Pilate heard them say this his fears increased. Re-entering the Praetorium, he said to Jesus, 'Where do you come from?' But Jesus made no answer. Pilate then said to him, 'Are you refusing to speak to me? Surely you know I have power to release you and I have power to crucify you?' 'You would have no power over me' replied Jesus 'if it had not been given you from above; that is why the one who handed me over to you has the greater guilt.'

From that moment Pilate was anxious to set him free, but the Jews shouted, **'If you set him free you are no friend of Caesar's; anyone who makes himself king is defying Caesar.'** Hearing these words, Pilate had Jesus brought out, and seated himself on the chair of judgement at a place called the Pavement, in Hebrew Gabbatha. It was Passover Preparation Day, about the sixth hour. 'Here is your king' said Pilate to the Jews. **'Take him away, take him away! Crucify him!'** they said. 'Do you want me to crucify your king? said Pilate. The chief priests answered, **'We have no king except Caesar.'** So in the end Pilate handed him over to them to be crucified.

They then took charge of Jesus, and carrying his own cross he went out of the city to the place of the skull or, as it was called in Hebrew, Golgotha, where they crucified him with two others, one on either side with Jesus in the middle. Pilate wrote out a notice and had it fixed to the cross; it ran: 'Jesus the Nazarene, King of the Jews.'

This notice was read by many of the Jews, because the place where Jesus was crucified was not far from the city, and the writing was in Hebrew, Latin and Greek. So the Jewish chief priests said to Pilate, **'You should not write "King of the Jews" but "This man said: I am King of the Jews".'** Pilate answered, 'What I have written, I have written.'

When the soldiers had finished crucifying Jesus they took his clothing and divided it into four shares, one for each soldier. His undergarment was seamless, woven in one piece from neck to hem; so they said to one another, **'Instead of tearing it, let's throw dice to decide who is to have it.'** In this way the words of scripture were fulfilled: They shared out my clothing among them. They cast lots for my clothes. This is exactly what the soldiers did.

Near the cross of Jesus stood his mother and his mother's sister, Mary the wife of Clopas, and Mary of Magdala. Seeing his mother and the disciple he loved standing near her, Jesus said to his mother, 'Woman, this is your son.' Then to the disciple he said, 'This is your mother.' And from that moment the disciple made a place for her in his home.

After this Jesus knew that everything had now been completed, and to fulfil the scripture perfectly he said: 'I am thirsty.'

A jar full of vinegar stood there, so putting a sponge soaked in the vinegar on a hyssop stick they held it up to his mouth. After Jesus had taken the vinegar he said, 'It is accomplished'; and bowing his head he gave up the spirit.

It was Preparation Day, and to prevent the bodies remaining on the cross during the sabbath—since that sabbath was a day of special solemnity—the Jews asked Pilate to have the legs broken and the bodies taken away. Consequently the soldiers came and broke the legs of the first man who had been crucified with him and then of the other. When they came to Jesus, they found he was already dead, and so instead of breaking his legs one of the soldiers pierced his side with a lance; and immediately there came out blood and water. This is the evidence of one who saw it—trustworthy evidence, and he knows he speaks the truth—and he gives it so that you may believe as well. Because all this happened to fulfil the words of scripture: Not one bone of his will be broken; and again, in another place scripture says: They will look on the one whom they have pierced. After this, Joseph of Arimathaea, who was a disciple of Jesus—though a secret one because he was afraid of the Jews—asked Pilate to let him remove the body of Jesus. Pilate gave permission, so they came and took it away. Nicodemus came as well—the same one who had first come to Jesus at night-time—and he brought a mixture of myrrh and aloes, weighing about a hundred pounds. They took the body of Jesus and wrapped it with the spices in linen cloths, following the Jewish burial custom. At the place where he had been crucified there was a garden, and in this garden a new tomb in which no one had yet been buried. Since it was the Jewish Day of Preparation and the tomb was near at hand, they laid Jesus there.

GENERAL INTERCESSIONS

1. For the Church

Let us pray, dear friends,
for the holy Church of God throughout
    the world,
that God the almighty Father

guide it and gather it together
so that we may worship him
in peace and tranquillity.

Silent prayer. Then
Almighty and eternal God,
you have shown your glory to all nations
in Christ, your Son.
Guide the work of your Church.
Help it to persevere in faith,
proclaim your name,
and bring your salvation to people everywhere.

2. For the Pope

Let us pray
for our Holy Father, Pope N.,
that God who chose him to be bishop
may give him health and strength
to guide and govern God's holy people.

Silent prayer. Then

Almighty and eternal God,
you guide all things by your word,
you govern all Christian people.
In your love protect the Pope you have chosen for us.
Under his leadership deepen our faith
and make us better Christians.

3. For the clergy and laity of the Church

Let us pray
for N., our bishop,
for all bishops, priests, and deacons;
for all who have a special ministry in the Church
and for all God's people.

Silent prayer. Then

Almighty and eternal God,
your Spirit guides the Church
and makes it holy.
Listen to our prayers
and help each of us
in his own vocation
to do your work more faithfully.

4. For those preparing for baptism

Let us pray
for those (among us) preparing for baptism,
that God in his mercy
make them responsive to his love,
forgive their sins through the waters of new birth,
and give them life in Jesus Christ our Lord.

Silent prayer. Then

Almighty and eternal God,
you continually bless your Church with new members.
Increase the faith and understanding
of those (among us) preparing for baptism.
Give them a new birth in these living waters
and make them members of your chosen family.

5. For the unity of Christians

Let us pray
for all our brothers and sisters
who share our faith in Jesus Christ,
that God may gather and keep together in one Church
all those who seek the truth with sincerity.
Silent prayer. Then
Almighty and eternal God,
you keep together those you have united.
Look kindly on all who follow Jesus your Son.
We are all consecrated to you by our common baptism.
Make us one in the fullness of faith,
and keep us one in the fellowship of love.

6. For the Jewish people

Let us pray
for the Jewish people,
the first to hear the word of God,
that they may continue to grow in the love of his name
and in faithfulness to his covenant.
Silent prayer. Then
Almighty and eternal God,
long ago you gave your promise to Abraham and his posterity.
Listen to your Church as we pray
that the people you first made your own
may arrive at the fullness of redemption.

7. For those who do not believe in Christ

Let us pray
for those who do not believe in Christ,
that the light of the Holy Spirit
may show them the way to salvation.
Silent prayer. Then
Almighty and eternal God,
enable those who do not acknowledge Christ
to find the truth
as they walk before you in sincerity of heart.
Help us to grow in love for one another,
to grasp more fully the mystery of your godhead,
and to become more perfect witnesses of your love
in the sight of men.

8. For those who do not believe in God

Let us pray
for those who do not believe in God,
that they may find him
by sincerely following all that is right.
Silent prayer. Then

Almighty and eternal God,
you created mankind
so that all might long to find you
and have peace when you are found.
Grant that, in spite of the hurtful things
that stand in their way,
they may all recognize in the lives of Christians
the tokens of your love and mercy,
and gladly acknowledge you
as the one true God and Father of us all.

9. For all in public office

Let us pray
for those who serve us in public office,
that God may guide their minds and hearts,
so that all men may live in true peace and freedom.
Silent prayer. Then

Almighty and eternal God,
you know the longings of men's hearts
and you protect their rights.
In your goodness
watch over those in authority,
so that people everywhere may enjoy
religious freedom, security, and peace.

10. For those in special need

Let us pray, dear friends,
that God the almighty Father
may heal the sick,
comfort the dying,
give safety to travellers,
free those unjustly deprived of liberty,
and rid the world of falsehood,
hunger, and disease.
Silent prayer. Then

Almighty, ever-living God,
you give strength to the weary
and new courage to those who have lost heart.
Hear the prayers of all who call on you in any trouble
that they may have the joy of receiving your help in their need.

SECOND PART: VENERATION OF THE CROSS
The priest says (or sings):

This is the wood of the cross, on which hung the Saviour of the world.

All reply:

Come, let us worship.

He does this three times and after each response all kneel and venerate the cross. The priest then places the cross in a suitable place and all the people approach it, making a simple genuflection or some other appropriate sign of reverence.

If the number of people present makes it impossible for everyone to venerate the cross individually, the priest may hold it up and invite everyone to worship in silence.

THIRD PART: COMMUNION
The Blessed Sacrament is brought from the Altar of Repose and the priest begins the Communion Rite Turn to page 24

PRAYER AFTER COMMUNION
Almighty and eternal God,
you have restored us to life
by the triumphant death and resurrection of Christ.
Continue this healing work within us.
May we who participate in this mystery
never cease to serve you.

The priest blesses the people as follows:

Lord,
send down your abundant blessing
upon your people who have devoutly recalled the death of your Son
in the sure hope of the resurrection.
Grant them pardon; bring them comfort.
May their faith grow stronger
and their eternal salvation be assured.
We ask this through Christ our Lord.
Amen.

All depart in silence. The altar is stripped at a convenient time.

Easter Vigil
FIRST PART: THE SERVICE OF LIGHT
All the lights in the church are put out and a large fire is prepared in a suitable place outside the church. When the people have assembled the priest goes there with the ministers, one of whom carries the Easter candle. The priest greets the congregation in the usual manner and briefly instructs them about the vigil in these or similar words:

Dear friends in Christ,
on this most holy night,
when our Lord Jesus Christ passed from death to life,
the Church invites her children throughout the world
to come together in vigil and prayer.
This is the passover of the Lord:
if we honour the memory of his death and resurrection

by hearing his word and celebrating his mysteries,
then we may be confident
that we shall share his victory over death
and live with him for ever in God.
Then the fire is blessed.

Let us pray.
Father,
we share in the light of your glory
through your Son, the light of the world.
Make this new fire + holy, and inflame us with new hope.
Purify our minds by this Easter celebration
and bring us one day to the feast of eternal light.

The Easter candle is lighted from the new fire. After the blessing of the new fire, an acolyte or one of the ministers brings the Easter candle to the celebrant, who cuts a cross in the wax with a stylus. Then he traces the Greek letter 'alpha' above the cross, the letter 'omega' below, and the numerals of the current year between the arms of the cross. Meanwhile he says:

Christ yesterday and today,
the beginning and the end,
Alpha,
and Omega;
all time belongs to him,
and all the ages;
to him be glory and power,
through every age for ever. Amen.

A
1 | 9
7
Ω

When the cross and other marks have been made, the priest may insert five grains of incense in the candle. He does this in the form of a cross saying:

By his holy
and glorious wounds
may Christ our Lord
guard us
and keep us. Amen.

The priest lights the candle from the new fire saying:

May the light of Christ, rising in glory,
dispel the darkness of our hearts and minds.

Then the priest takes the candle, lifts it high, and sings:

Christ our light.
Thanks be to God.

He does this twice more during the procession.

EASTER PROCLAMATION (EXSULTET)

The Easter candle is placed on the stand in the middle of the sanctuary. The deacon, or priest, sings the Easter proclamation. All stand and hold lighted candles.

Rejoice, heavenly powers! Sing, choirs of angels!
    Exult, all creation around God's throne!
    Jesus Christ, our King, is risen!
    Sound the trumpet of salvation!

Rejoice, O earth, in shining splendour,
   radiant in the brightness of your King!
Christ has conquered! Glory fills you!
Darkness vanishes for ever!
Rejoice, O Mother Church! Exult in glory!
   The risen Saviour shines upon you!
Let this place resound with joy,
   echoing the mighty song of all God's people!
(My dearest friends, standing with me in this holy light,
   join me in asking God for mercy,
   that he may give his unworthy minister
   grace to sing his Easter praises.)
(The Lord be with you.
And also with you.)
Lift up your hearts.
We lift them up to the Lord.
Let us give thanks to the Lord our God.
It is right to give him thanks and praise.

It is truly right
that with full hearts and minds and voices
we should praise the unseen God, the all-powerful Father,
and his only Son, our Lord Jesus Christ.
For Christ has ransomed us with his blood,
   and paid for us the price of Adam's sin
   to our eternal Father!
This is our passover feast,
   when Christ, the true Lamb, is slain,
   whose blood consecrates the homes of all believers.
This is the night when first you saved our fathers:
   you freed the people of Israel from their slavery
   and led them dry-shod through the sea.
This is the night when the pillar of fire
   destroyed the darkness of sin!
This is the night when Christians everywhere,
   washed clean of sin
   and freed from all defilement,
   are restored to grace and grow together in holiness.
This is the night when Jesus Christ
   broke the chains of death
   and rose triumphant from the grave.
What good would life have been to us,
   had Christ not come as our Redeemer?
Father, how wonderful your care for us!
   How boundless your merciful love!
   To ransom a slave
   you gave away your Son.
O happy fault, O necessary sin of Adam,
   which gained for us so great a Redeemer!

Most blessed of all nights, chosen by God
　to see Christ rising from the dead!
Of this night scripture says:
　"The night will be as clear as day:
　it will become my light, my joy."
The power of this holy night
　dispels all evil, washes guilt away,
　restores lost innocence, bring mourners joy;
　it casts out hatred, brings us peace, and humbles earthly pride.
Night truly blessed when heaven is wedded to earth
　and man is reconciled with God!
Therefore, heavenly Father, in the joy of this night,
　receive our evening sacrifice of praise,
　your Church's solemn offering.
Accept this Easter candle,
　a flame divided but undimmed,
　a pillar of fire that glows to the honour of God.
Let it mingle with the lights of heaven
　and continue bravely burning
　to dispel the darkness of this night!
May the Morning Star which never sets find this flame still burning:
　Christ, the Morning Star, who came back from the dead,
　and shed his peaceful light on all mankind,
　your Son who lives and reigns for ever and ever.
Amen.

SECOND PART: LITURGY OF THE WORD

After the Easter proclamation the candles are put out and all sit down. Before the readings the priest speaks to the people in these or similar words:

Dear friends in Christ,
we have begun our solemn vigil.
Let us now listen attentively to the Word of God,
recalling how he saved his people throughout history
and, in the fullness of time,
sent his own Son to be our Redeemer.
Through this Easter celebration,
may God bring to perfection
the saving work he has begun in us.

FIRST READING　　　　　　　　　　　　　　　　　*Genesis 1:1-2:2*

God saw all he had made, and indeed it was very good.

In the beginning God created the heavens and the earth. Now the earth was a formless void, there was darkness over the deep, and God's spirit hovered over the water.

God said, 'Let there be light,' and there was light. God saw the light was good, and God divided light from darkness. God called the light 'day', and darkness he called 'night'. Evening came and morning came: the first day.

God said, 'Let there be a vault in the waters to divide the waters in two.' And so it was. God made the vault, and it divided the waters above the vault from the waters under the vault. God called the vault 'heaven'. Evening came and morning came: the second day.

God said, 'Let the waters under heaven come together into a single mass, and let dry land appear.' And so it was. God called the dry land 'earth' and the mass of waters 'seas', and God saw that it was good.

God said, 'Let the earth produce vegetation: seed-bearing plants, and fruit trees bearing fruit with their seed inside, on the earth.' And so it was. The earth produced vegetation, plants bearing seed in their several kinds, and trees bearing fruit with their seed inside in their several kinds. God saw that it was good. Evening came and morning came: the third day.

God said, 'Let there be lights in the vault of heaven to divide day from night, and let them indicate festivals, days and years. Let them be lights in the vault of heaven to shine on the earth.' And so it was. God made the two great lights: the greater light to govern the day, the smaller light to govern the night, and the stars. God set them in the vault of heaven to shine on the earth, to govern the day and the night and to divide light from darkness. God saw that it was good. Evening came and morning came: the fourth day.

God said, 'Let the waters teem with living creatures, and let birds fly above the earth within the vault of heaven.' And so it was. God created great sea-serpents and every kind of living creature with which the waters teem, and every kind of winged creature. God saw that it was good. God blessed them saying 'Be fruitful, multiply, and fill the waters of the seas; and let the birds multiply upon the earth.' Evening came and morning came: the fifth day.

God said, 'Let the earth produce every kind of living creature: cattle, reptiles, and every kind of wild beast.' And so it was. God made every kind of wild beast, every kind of cattle, and every kind of land reptile. God saw that it was good.

God said, 'Let us make man in our own image, in the likeness of ourselves, and let them be masters of the fish of the sea, the birds of heaven, the cattle, all the wild beasts and all the reptiles that crawl upon the earth.'

God created man in the image of himself, in the image of God he created him, male and female he created them.

God blessed them, saying to them, 'Be fruitful, multiply, fill the earth and conquer it. Be masters of the fish of the sea, the birds of heaven and all living animals on the earth.' God said, 'See, I give you all the seed-bearing plants that are upon the whole earth, and all the trees with seed-bearing fruit; this shall be your food. To all wild beasts, all birds of heaven and all living reptiles on the earth I give all the foliage of plants for food.' And so it was. God saw all he had made, and indeed it was very good. Evening came and morning came: the sixth day.

Thus heaven and earth were completed with all their array. On the seventh day God completed the work he had been doing. He rested on the seventh day after all the work he had been doing.

This is the word of the Lord. **Thanks be to God.**

RESPONSORIAL PSALM   *Ps 103:1-2, 5-6, 10, 12-14, 24, 35.R.v.30*
Send forth your spirit, O Lord, and renew the face of the earth.

1. Bless the Lord, my soul!
Lord God, how great you are,
clothed in majesty and glory,
wrapped in light as in a robe!
2. You founded the earth on its base,
to stand firm from age to age.
You wrapped it with the ocean like a
   cloak;
the waters stood higher than the
   mountains.

3. You make the springs gush forth in
   the valleys:
they flow in between the hills.
On their banks dwell the birds of
   heaven;
from the branches they sing their song.
4. From your dwelling you water the
   hills;
earth drinks its fill of your gift.
You make the grass grow for the cattle
and the plants to serve man's needs.

5. How many are your works, O Lord!
In wisdom you have made them all.
The earth is full of your riches.
Bless the Lord, my soul!

All stand for the prayer.
Almighty and eternal God,
you created all things in wonderful beauty and order.
Help us now to perceive
how still more wonderful is the new creation
by which in the fullness of time
you redeemed your people
through the sacrifice of our passover, Jesus Christ,
who lives and reigns for ever and ever. **Amen.**

SECOND READING   *Genesis 22:1-18*
The sacrifice of Abraham, our father in faith.
God put Abraham to the test. 'Abraham, Abraham,' he called. 'Here I am' he
replied. 'Take your son,' God said 'your only child Isaac, whom you love, and go to
the land of Moriah. There you shall offer him as a burnt offering, on a mountain I
will point out to you.'
Rising early next morning Abraham saddled his ass and took with him two of his
servants and his son Isaac. He chopped wood for the burnt offering and started on
his journey to the place God had pointed out to him. On the third day Abraham
looked up and saw the place in the distance. Then Abraham said to his servants,
'Stay here with the donkey. The boy and I will go over there; we will worship and
come back to you.'
Abraham took the wood for the burnt offering, loaded it on Isaac, and carried in his
own hands the fire and the knife. Then the two of them set out together. Isaac spoke
to his father Abraham, 'Father', he said. 'Yes, my son,' he replied. 'Look,' he said
'here are the fire and the wood, but where is the lamb for the burnt offering?'
Abraham answered, 'My son, God himself will provide the lamb for the burnt
offering.' Then the two of them went on together.
When they arrived at the place God had pointed out to him, Abraham built an altar
there, and arranged the wood. Then he bound his son Isaac and put him on the altar
on top of the wood. Abraham stretched out his hand and seized the knife to kill his
son.
But the angel of the Lord called to him from heaven. 'Abraham, Abraham' he said.

'I am here' he replied. 'Do not raise your hand against the boy' the angel said. 'Do not harm him, for now I know you fear God. You have not refused me your son, your only son.' Then looking up, Abraham saw a ram caught by its horns in a bush. Abraham took the ram and offered it as a burnt offering in place of his son. Abraham called this place 'The Lord provides', and hence the saying today: On the mountain the Lord provides. The angel of the Lord called Abraham a second time from heaven. 'I swear by my own self—it is the Lord who speaks—because you have done this, because you have not refused me your son, your only son, I will shower blessings on you, I will make your descendants as many as the stars of heaven and the grains of sand on the seashore. Your descendants shall gain possession of the gates of their enemies. All the nations of the earth shall bless themselves by your descendants, as a reward for your obedience.'
This is the word of the Lord. **Thanks be to God.**

RESPONSORIAL PSALM   *Psalm 15:5, 8-11. R.v.1*

Preserve me, God, I take refuge in you.

1. O Lord, it is you who are my portion and cup;
it is you yourself who are my prize.
I keep the Lord ever in my sight:
since he is at my right hand, I shall stand firm.

2. And so my heart rejoices, my soul is glad;
even my body shall rest in safety.
For you will not leave my soul among the dead,
nor let your beloved know decay.

3. You will show me the path of life,
the fullness of joy in your presence,
at your right hand happiness for ever.

All stand for the prayer.
God and Father of all who believe in you,
you promised Abraham that he would become the father of all nations,
and through the death and resurrection of Christ
you fulfil that promise:
everywhere throughout the world you increase your chosen people.
May we respond to your call
by joyfully accepting your invitation to the new life of grace.

THIRD READING   *Exodus 14:15-15:1*

The sons of Israel went on dry ground right into the sea.

The Lord said to Moses, 'Why do you cry to me so? Tell the sons of Israel to march on. For yourself, raise your staff and stretch out your hand over the sea and part it for the sons of Israel to walk through the sea on dry ground. I for my part will make the heart of the Egyptians so stubborn that they will follow them. So shall I win myself glory at the expense of the Pharaoh, of all his army, his chariots, his horsemen. And when I have won glory for myself, at the expense of Pharoah and his chariots and his army, the Egyptians will learn that I am the Lord.'
Then the angel of the Lord, who marched at the front of the army of Israel, changed station and moved to their rear. The pillar of cloud changed station from the front to the rear of them, and remained there. It came between the camp of the Egyptians and the camp of Israel. The cloud was dark, and the night passed without the armies drawing any closer the whole night long. Moses stretched out his hand over the sea. The Lord drove back the sea with a strong easterly wind all night, and he made dry

land of the sea. The waters parted and the sons of Israel went on dry ground right into the sea, walls of water to right and left of them. The Egyptians gave chase: after them they went, right into the sea, all Pharaoh's horses, his chariots, and his horsemen. In the morning watch, the Lord looked down on the army of the Egyptians from the pillar of fire and of cloud, and threw the army into confusion. He so clogged their chariot wheels that they could scarcely make headway. 'Let us flee from the Israelites,' the Egyptians cried 'the Lord is fighting for them against the Egyptians!' 'Stretch out your hand over the sea,' the Lord said to Moses 'that the waters may flow back on the Egyptians and their chariots and their horsemen.' Moses stretched out his hand over the sea and, as day broke, the sea returned to its bed. The fleeing Egyptians marched right into it, and the Lord overthrew the Egyptians in the very middle of the sea. The returning waters overwhelmed the chariots and the horsemen of Pharaoh's whole army, which had followed the Israelites into the sea; not a single one of them was left. But the sons of Israel had marched through the sea on dry ground, walls of water to right and to left of them. That day, the Lord rescued Israel from the Egyptians, and Israel saw the Egyptians lying dead on the shore. Israel witnessed the great act that the Lord had performed against the Egyptians, and the people venerated the Lord; they put their faith in the Lord and in Moses, his servant.

It was then that Moses and the sons of Israel sang this song in honour of the lord:

RESPONSORIAL PSALM   *Exodus 15:1-6, 17-18. R.v.1*
I will sing to the Lord, glorious his triumph!
1. I will sing to the Lord, glorious his triumph!
   Horse and rider he has thrown into the sea!
   The Lord is my strength, my song, my salvation.
   This is my God and I extol him,
   my father's God and I give him praise.
2. The Lord is a warrior! The Lord is his name.
   The chariots of Pharaoh he hurled into the sea,
   the flower of his army is drowned in the sea.
   The deeps hide them; they sank like a stone.
3. Your right hand, Lord, glorious in its power,
   your right hand, Lord, has shattered the enemy.
   In the greatness of your glory you crushed
   the foe.
4. You will lead them and plant them on your mountain,
   the place, O Lord, where you have made your home,
   the sanctuary, Lord, which your hands have made.
   The Lord will reign for ever and ever.

All stand for the prayer.

Father,
even today we see the wonders
of the miracles you worked long ago.
You once saved a single nation from slavery,
and now you offer that salvation to all through baptism.
May the peoples of the world become true sons of Abraham
and prove worthy of the heritage of Israel.

FOURTH READING   *Isaiah 54:5-14*

With everlasting love the Lord your redeemer has taken pity on you.

For now your creator will be your husband, his name, the Lord of hosts; your redeemer will be the Holy One of Israel, he is called the God of the whole earth. Yes, like a forsaken wife, distressed in spirit, the Lord calls you back. Does a man cast off the wife of his youth? says your God. I did forsake you for a brief moment, but with great love will I take you back. In excess of anger, for a moment I hid my face from you. But with everlasting love I have taken pity on you, says the Lord, your redeemer.

I am now as I was in the days of Noah when I swore that Noah's waters should never flood the world again. So now I swear concerning my anger with you and the threats I made against you; for the mountains may depart, the hills be shaken, but my love for you will never leave you and my covenant of peace with you will never be shaken, says the Lord who takes pity on you.

Unhappy creature, storm-tossed, disconsolate, see, I will set your stones on carbuncles and your foundations on sapphires. I will make rubies your battlements, your gates crystal, and your entire wall precious stones. Your sons will all be taught by the Lord. The prosperity of your sons will be great. You will be founded on integrity; remote from oppression, you will have nothing to fear; remote from terror, it will not approach you.

This is the word of the Lord. **Thanks be to God.**

RESPONSORIAL PSALM   *Psalm 29:2, 4-6, 11-13. R.v.2*

I will praise you, Lord, you have rescued me.

1. I will praise you, Lord, you have rescued me
   and have not let my enemies rejoice over me.
   O Lord, you have raised my soul from the dead,
   restored me to life from those who sink into the grave.

2. Sing psalms to the Lord, you who love him,
   give thanks to his holy name.
   His anger lasts but a moment; his favour through life.
   At night there are tears, but joy comes with dawn.

3. The Lord listened and had pity.
   The Lord came to my help.
   For me you have changed my mourning into dancing,
   O Lord my God, I will thank you for ever.

All stand for the prayer.

Almighty and eternal God,
glorify your name by increasing your chosen people
as you promised long ago.
In reward for their trust,
may we see in the Church the fulfilment of your promise.

FIFTH READING   *Isaiah 55:1-11*

Come to me and your soul will live, and I will make an everlasting covenant with you.

Thus says the Lord: Oh, come to the water all you who are thirsty; though you have no money, come! Buy corn without money, and eat, and, at no cost, wine and milk. Why spend money on what is not bread, your wages on what fails to satisfy? Listen,

listen to me, and you will have good things to eat and rich food to enjoy. Pay attention, come to me; listen, and your souls will live.
With you I will make an everlasting covenant out of the favours promised to David. See, I have made of you a witness to the peoples, a leader and a master of the nations. See, you will summon a nation you never knew, those unknown will come hurrying to you, for the sake of the Lord your God, of the Holy One of Israel who will glorify you.
Seek the Lord while he is still to be found, call to him while he is still near. Let the wicked man abandon his way, the evil man his thoughts. Let him turn back to the Lord who will take pity on him, to our God who is rich in forgiving; for my thoughts are not your thoughts, my ways not your ways—it is the Lord who speaks. Yes, the heavens are as high above earth as my ways are above your ways, my thoughts above your thoughts.
Yes, as the rain and the snow come down from the heavens and do not return without watering the earth, making it yield and giving growth to provide seed for the sower and bread for the eating, so the word that goes from my mouth does not return to me empty, without carrying out my will and succeeding in what it was sent to do.
This is the word of the Lord. **Thanks be to God.**

RESPONSORIAL PSALM   *Isaiah 12:2, 6.R.v.3*
With joy you will draw water from the wells of salvation.
1. Truly God is my salvation,   2. Give thanks to the Lord, give praise
I trust, I shall not fear.   to his name!
For the Lord is my strength, my song,   Make his mighty deeds known to the
he became my saviour.   peoples,
With joy you will draw water   declare the greatness of his name.
from the wells of salvation.

3. Sing a psalm to the Lord
for he has done glorious deeds,
make them known to all the earth!
People of Zion, sing and shout for joy
for great in your midst is the Holy One of Israel.

All stand for the prayer.
Almighty, ever-living God,
only hope of the world,
by the preaching of the prophets
you proclaimed the mysteries we are celebrating tonight.
Help us to be your faithful people,
for it is by your inspiration alone
that we can grow in goodness.

SIXTH READING   *Baruch 3:9-15, 32-4:4*
In the radiance of the Lord make your way to light.
Listen, Israel, to commands that bring life; hear, and learn what knowledge means,
Why, Israel, why are you in the country of your enemies, growing older and older in an alien land, sharing defilement with the dead, reckoned with those who go to Sheol? Because you have forsaken the fountain of wisdom. Had you walked in the way of God, you would have lived in peace for ever. Learn where knowledge is,

where strength, where understanding, and so learn where length of days is, where life, where the light of the eyes and where peace. But who has found out where she lives, who has entered her treasure house?

But the One who knows all knows her, he has grasped her with his own intellect, he has set the earth firm for ever and filled it with four-footed beasts, he sends the light—and it goes, he recalls it—and trembling it obeys; the stars shine joyfully at their set times: when he calls them, they answer, 'Here we are'; they gladly shine for their creator. It is he who is our God, no other can compare with him. He has grasped the whole way of knowledge, and confided it to his servant Jacob, to Israel his well-beloved; so causing her to appear on earth and move among men.

This is the book of the commandments of God, the Law that stands for ever; those who desert her die. Turn back, Jacob, seize her, in her radiance make your way to light: do not yield your glory to another, your privilege to a people not your own. Israel, blessed are we: what pleases God has been revealed to us.

This is the word of the Lord. **Thanks be to God.**

RESPONSORIAL PSALM
Psalm 18:8-11. R.Jn 6:69

You have the message of eternal life, O Lord.

1. The Law of the Lord is perfect,
it revives the soul.
The rule of the Lord is to be trusted,
it gives wisdom to the simple.

2. The precepts of the Lord are right,
they gladden the heart.
The command of the Lord is clear,
it gives light to the eyes.

3. The fear of the Lord is holy,
abiding for ever.
The decrees of the Lord are truth
and all of them just.

4. They are more to be desired than gold,
than the purest of gold
and sweeter are they than honey,
than honey from the comb.

All stand for the prayer.

Father,
you increase your Church
by continuing to call all people to salvation.
Listen to our prayers
and always watch over those you cleanse in baptism.

SEVENTH READING
Ezekiel 36:16-28

I shall pour clean water over you, and I shall give you a new heart.

The word of the Lord was addressed to me as follows: 'Son of man, the members of the House of Israel used to live in their own land, but they defiled it by their conduct and actions. I then discharged my fury at them because of the blood they shed in their land and the idols with which they defiled it. I scattered them among the nations and dispersed them in foreign countries. I sentenced them as their conduct and actions deserved. And now they have profaned my holy name among the nations where they have gone, so that people say of them. "These are the people of the Lord; they have been exiled from his land." But I have been concerned about my holy name, which the House of Israel has profaned among the nations where they have gone. And so, say to the House of Israel, "The Lord says this: I am not doing this for your sake, House of Israel, but for the sake of my holy name, which you have profaned among the nations where you have gone. I mean to display the holiness of my great name, which has been profaned among the nations, which you have profaned among them. And the nations will learn that I am the Lord—it is the Lord who speaks—when I display my holiness for your sake before their eyes. Then I am going to take you from among the nations and gather you together from all the foreign countries, and bring you home to your own land. I shall pour clean water over you and you will be cleansed; I shall cleanse you of all your defilement and all your idols. I shall give you a new heart, and put a new spirit in you; I shall remove the heart of stone from your bodies and give you a heart of flesh instead. I shall put my spirit in you, and make you keep my laws and sincerely respect my observances. You will live in the land which I gave your ancestors. You shall be my people and I will be your God." '

This is the word of the Lord. **Thanks be to God.**

RESPONSORIAL PSALM   *Psalms 41:3, 5, 42:3, 4.R.41:2*

Like the deer that yearns for running streams so my soul is yearning for you, my God.

1. My soul is thirsting for God,
the God of my life;
when can I enter and see
the face of God?

2. These things will I remember
as I pour out my soul:
how I would lead the rejoicing crowd
into the house of God,
amid cries of gladness and thanksgiving,
the throng wild with joy.

3. O send forth your light and your
truth;
let these be my guide.
Let them bring me to your holy
mountain to the place where you
dwell.

4. And I will come to the altar of God,
the God of my joy.
My redeemer, I will thank you on the
harp,
O God, my God.

All stand for the prayer.

God of unchanging power and light,
look with mercy and favour on your entire Church.
Bring lasting salvation to mankind,
so that the world may see
the fallen lifted up,
the old made new,
and all things brought to perfection,
through him who is their origin,
our Lord Jesus Christ,
who lives and reigns for ever and ever.

Or, if anyone is to be baptised:
Almighty and eternal God,
be present in this sacrament of your love.
Send your spirit of adoption
on those to be born again in baptism.
And may the work of our humble ministry
be brought to perfection by your mighty power.

| Turn to page 6 for the Gloria |

OPENING PRAYER OF THE MASS

Lord God,
you have brightened this night
with the radiance of the risen Christ.

Quicken the spirit of sonship in your Church;
renew us in mind and body
to give you whole-hearted service.
Grant this through our Lord Jesus Christ, your Son,
who lives and reigns with you and the Holy Spirit,
one God, for ever and ever.
Amen.

EPISTLE   *Romans 6:3-11*

A reading from the letter of St Paul to the Romans.

Christ, having been raised from the dead, will never die again.

You have been taught that when we were baptised in Christ Jesus we were baptised
in his death; in other words, when we were baptised we went into the tomb with him
and joined him in death, so that as Christ was raised from the dead by the Father's
glory, we too might live a new life. If in union with Christ we have imitated his death,
we shall also imitate him in his resurrection. We must realise that our former selves
have been crucified with him to destroy this sinful body and to free us from the
slavery of sin. When a man dies, of course, he has finished with sin.
But we believe that having died with Christ we shall return to life with him: Christ,
as we know, having been raised from the dead will never die again. Death has no
power over him any more. When he died, he died, once for all, to sin, so his life now
is life with God; and in that way, you too must consider yourselves to be dead to sin
but alive for God in Christ Jesus.
This is the word of the Lord. **Thanks be to God.**

*All now rise to greet the Gospel, and the priest or cantor intones the 'Alleluia' which is
repeated by all present.*

                                                    Ps 117:1-2, 16-17, 22-23

Alleluia, alleluia, alleluia!

1. Alleluia!   2. The Lord's right hand has
Give thanks to the Lord for he is good,   triumphed;
for his love has no end.   his right hand raised me up.
Let the sons of Israel say: I shall not die, I shall live
'His love has no end.'   and recount his deeds.

                    3. The stone which the builders rejected
                    has become the corner stone.
                    This is the work of the Lord,
                    a marvel in our eyes.

THE GOSPEL   *Luke 24:1-12*

The Lord be with you. **And also with you.**
A reading from the holy Gospel according to Luke. **Glory to you, Lord.**

Why look among the dead for someone who is alive?

On the first day of the week, at the first sign of dawn, they went to the tomb with the
spices they had prepared. They found that the stone had been rolled away from the
tomb, but on entering discovered that the body of the Lord Jesus was not there. As
they stood there not knowing what to think, two men in brilliant clothes suddenly
appeared at their side. Terrified, the women lowered their eyes. But the two men said
to them, "Why look among the dead for someone who is alive? He is not here; he

has risen. Remember what he told you when he was still in Galilee: that the Son of Man had to be handed over into the power of sinful men and be crucified, and rise again on the third day?" And they remembered his words.

When the women returned from the tomb they told all this to the Eleven and to all the others. The women were Mary of Magdala, Joanna, and Mary the mother of James. The other women with them also told the apostles, but this story of theirs seemed pure nonsense, and they did not believe them.

Peter, however, went running to the tomb. He bent down and saw the binding cloths, but nothing else; he then went back home, amazed at what had happened. This is the Gospel of the Lord. **Praise to you, Lord Jesus Christ.**

The Homily may follow.

PART THREE: LITURGY OF BAPTISM

The priest with the ministers goes to the baptismal font if this can be seen by the congregation. Otherwise a vessel of water is placed in the sanctuary. If there are candidates to be baptised they are called forward.

Dear friends in Christ,
as our brothers and sisters approach the waters of rebirth,
let us help them by our prayers
and ask God, our almighty Father,
to support them with his mercy and love.

If the font is to be blessed, but there is no one to be baptised

Dear friends in Christ,
let us ask God, the almighty Father,
to bless this font,
that those reborn in it
may be made one with his adopted children in Christ.

THE LITANY

All stand.

Lord, have mercy	**Lord, have mercy**
Christ, have mercy	**Christ, have mercy**
Lord, have mercy	**Lord, have mercy**
Holy Mary, Mother of God	**pray for us**
Saint Michael	**pray for us**
Holy angels of God	**pray for us**
Saint John the Baptist	**pray for us**
Saint Joseph	**pray for us**
Saint Peter and Saint Paul	**pray for us**
Saint Andrew	**pray for us**
Saint John	**pray for us**
Saint Mary Magdalene	**pray for us**
Saint Stephen	**pray for us**
Saint Ignatius	**pray for us**
Saint Lawrence	**pray for us**
Saint Perpetua and Saint Felicity	**pray for us**
Saint Agnes	**pray for us**
Saint Gregory	**pray for us**

Saint Augustine	**pray for us**
Saint Athanasius	**pray for us**
Saint Basil	**pray for us**
Saint Martin	**pray for us**
Saint Benedict	**pray for us**
Saint Francis and Saint Dominic	**pray for us**
Saint Francis Xavier	**pray for us**
Saint John Vianney	**pray for us**
Saint Catherine	**pray for us**
Saint Teresa	**pray for us**
All holy men and women	**pray for us**
Lord, be merciful	**Lord, save your people**
From all evil	**Lord, save your people**
From every sin	**Lord, save your people**
From everlasting death	**Lord, save your people**
⟩ By your coming as man	**Lord, save your people**
By your death and rising to new life	**Lord, save your people**
By your gift of the Holy Spirit	**Lord, save your people**
Be merciful to us sinners	**Lord, hear our prayer**

If there are candidates to be baptised
Give new life to those chosen ones by the grace of
   baptism   **Lord, hear our prayer**

If there is no one to be baptised
By your grace bless this font where your children

will be reborn	**Lord, hear our prayer**
Jesus, Son of the living God	**Lord, hear our prayer**
Christ, hear us	**Christ, hear us**
Lord Jesus, hear our prayer	**Lord Jesus, hear our prayer**

BLESSING OF WATER

The priest then blesses the baptismal water.

Father, you give us grace through sacramental signs,
   which tell us of the wonders of your unseen power.

In baptism we use your gift of water,
   which you have made a rich symbol
   of the grace you give us in this sacrament.

At the very dawn of creation
   your Spirit breathed on the waters,
   making them the wellspring of all holiness.

The waters of the great flood
   you made a sign of the waters of baptism,
   that make an end of sin and a new beginning of goodness.

Through the waters of the Red Sea
   you led Israel out of slavery,
   to be an image of God's holy people,
   set free from sin by baptism.

In the waters of the Jordan
  your son was baptised by John
  and anointed with the Spirit.

Your Son willed that water and blood
  should flow from his side
  as he hung upon the cross.

After his resurrection he told his disciples:
  "Go out and teach all nations,
  baptising them in the name of the Father
  and of the Son and of the Holy Spirit."

Father, look now with love upon your Church,
  and unseal for her the fountain of baptism.

By the power of the Spirit
  give to the water of this font
  the grace of your Son.

You created man in your own likeness:
  cleanse him from sin in a new birth of innocence
  by water and the Spirit.

The priest may lower the Easter candle into the water either once or three times, as he continues:

We ask you, Father, with your Son
  to send the Holy Spirit upon the waters of this font.

He holds the candle in the water.

May all who are buried with Christ
  in the death of baptism
  rise also with him to newness of life.

Then the candle is taken out of the water as the people sing this or another acclamation:

Springs of water, bless the Lord.
Give him glory and praise for ever.

When the water has been blessed those awaiting baptism are baptised, first the adults and then the babies. Adult baptism begins with the renunciation of the devil and profession of faith by the candidates for baptism. The parents and godparents do this on behalf of the babies. Adults are confirmed immediately after baptism if a bishop or a priest with faculty to confirm is present. If no one is to be baptised and the font is not to be blessed, the priest blesses the water with the following prayer:

My brothers and sisters,
let us ask the Lord our God
to bless this water he has created,
which we shall use to recall our baptism.
May he renew us
and keep us faithful to the Spirit
we have all received.

All pray silently for a short while.

Lord our God,
this night your people keep prayerful vigil.

Be with us as we recall the wonder of our creation
and the greater wonder of our redemption.
Bless this water: it makes the seed to grow,
it refreshes us and makes us clean.
You have made of it a servant of your loving kindness:
through water you set your people free,
and quench their thirst in the desert.
With water the prophets announced a new covenant
that you would make with man.
By water, made holy by Christ in the Jordan,
you made our sinful nature new
in the bath that gives rebirth.
Let this water remind us of our baptism;
let us share the joys of our brothers
who are baptised this Easter.

RENEWAL OF BAPTISMAL PROMISES

When the rite of baptism (and confirmation) has been completed, or if there is no baptism, immediately after the blessing of the water, all present stand with lighted candles and renew their baptismal profession of faith. The priest speaks to the people in these or similar words:

Dear friends,
through the paschal mystery
we have been buried with Christ in baptism,
so that we may rise with him to a new life.
Now that we have completed our lenten observance,
let us renew the promises we made in baptism
when we rejected Satan and his works,
and promised to serve God faithfully
in his holy Catholic Church.
And so:

Do you reject Satan? **I do.**

And all his works? **I do.**

And all his empty promises? **I do.**

or:

Do you reject sin, so as to live in the freedom of God's children? **I do.**

Do you reject the glamour of evil, and refuse to be mastered by sin? **I do.**

Do you reject Satan, father of sin and prince of darkness? **I do.**

Then the priest continues:

Do you believe in God, the Father almighty,
creator of heaven and earth? **I do.**

Do you believe in Jesus Christ, his only Son, our Lord,
who was born of the Virgin Mary,
was crucified, died, and was buried,
rose from the dead,
and is now seated at the right hand of the Father? **I do.**

Do you believe in the Holy Spirit,
the holy Catholic Church, the communion of saints,
the forgiveness of sins, the resurrection of the body,
and life everlasting? **I do.**
God, the all-powerful Father of our Lord Jesus Christ,
has given us a new birth by water and the Holy Spirit,
and forgiven all our sins.
May he also keep us faithful to our Lord Jesus Christ for ever and ever. **Amen.**
The priest sprinkles the people with the blessed water, while all sing 'I saw water' or another song which is baptismal in character.

**I saw water flowing
from the right side of the temple, alleluia.
It brought God's life and his salvation,
and the people sang in joyful praise:
alleluia, alleluia.**

Meanwhile the newly baptised are led to their place among the faithful.

PART FOUR: LITURGY OF THE EUCHARIST

Turn to page 7 for the Offertory Prayers

PRAYER OVER THE GIFTS
Lord,
accept the prayers and offerings of your people.
With your help
may this Easter mystery of our redemption
bring to perfection the saving work you have begun in us.

Turn to page 14 for the Preface of Easter 1

COMMUNION ANTIPHON
Christ has become our paschal sacrifice; let us feast with the unleavened bread of sincerity and truth, alleluia.

PRAYER AFTER COMMUNION
Lord,
you have nourished us with your Easter sacraments.
Fill us with your Spirit,
and make us one in peace and love.

Turn to page 25 for the Concluding Rite

Easter Sunday

As the priest goes to the altar everyone joins in this Entrance Antiphon or a hymn.

I have risen: I am with you once more; you placed your hand on me to keep me safe. How great is the depth of your wisdom, alleluia!

Turn to page 4

**I have risen; I am still with you.
You have laid your hand upon me.
Your watchfulness over me has filled me with wonder,
alleluia.**

OPENING PRAYER

God our Father,
by raising Christ your Son
you conquered the power of death
and opened for us the way to eternal life.
Let our celebration today
raise us up and renew our lives
by the Spirit that is within us.

O God, today, through your only Son,
you conquered death and unlocked the
gates of eternal life. Grant that, as we
celebrate our Lord's resurrection, we
too may rise again in your light and the
new life of your Spirit.

FIRST READING   *Acts 10:34, 37-43*

We have eaten and drunk with him after his resurrection.

Peter addressed them: "You must have heard about the recent happenings in
Judaea; about Jesus of Nazareth and how he began in Galilee, after John had been
preaching baptism. God had anointed him with the Holy Spirit and with power, and
because God was with him, Jesus went about doing good and curing all who had
fallen into the power of the devil. Now I, and those with me, can witness to
everything he did throughout the countryside of Judaea and in Jerusalem itself: and
also to the fact that they killed him by hanging him on a tree, yet three days
afterwards God raised him to life and allowed him to be seen, not by the whole
people but only by certain witnesses God had chosen beforehand. Now we are those
witnesses—we have eaten and drunk with him after his resurrection from the
dead—and he has ordered us to proclaim this to his people and to tell them that God
has appointed him to judge everyone, alive or dead. It is to him that all the prophets
bear this witness: that all who believe in Jesus will have their sins forgiven through
his name."
This is the word of the Lord. **Thanks be to God.**

RESPONSORIAL PSALM   *Psalm 117*

This day was made by the Lord; we rejoice and are glad. *or:* **Alleluia!**

1. Alleluia.
Give thanks to the Lord for he is good,
for his love has no end.
Let the sons of Israel say:
"His love has no end."

2. The Lord's right hand has
   triumphed;
his right hand raised me up.
I shall not die, I shall live
and recount his deeds.

3. The stone which the builders rejected
has become the corner stone.
This is the work of the Lord,
a marvel in our eyes.

SECOND READING   *Colossians 3:1-4*

You must look for the things that are in heaven, where Christ is.

Since you have been brought back to true life with Christ, you must look for the
things that are in heaven, where Christ is, sitting at God's right hand. Let your
thoughts be on heavenly things, not on the things that are on the earth, because you
have died, and now the life you have is hidden with Christ in God but when Christ is
revealed—and he is your life—you too will be revealed in all your glory with him.
This is the word of the Lord. **Thanks be to God.**

SEQUENCE

Christians, to the Paschal Victim offer sacrifice and praise.
The sheep are ransomed by the Lamb;
and Christ, the undefiled,
hath sinners to his Father reconciled.
Death with life contended: combat strangely ended!
Life's own Champion, slain, yet lives to reign.
Tell us, Mary: say what thou didst see upon the way.
The tomb the Living did enclose;
I saw christ's glory as he rose!
These angels there attesting;
shroud with grave-clothes resting.
Christ, my hope, has risen: he goes before you into Galilee.
That Christ is truly risen from the dead we know.
Victorious king, thy mercy show!
Amen.

All stand to greet the Gospel. If this Acclamation is not sung it may be omitted.
Alleluia, alleluia! Christ, our passover, has been sacrificed; let us celebrate the feast
then, in the Lord. Alleluia!

THE GOSPEL   *John 20:1-9*

The Lord be with you. **And also with you.**
A reading from the holy Gospel according to John. **Glory to you, Lord.**

He must rise from the dead.

It was very early on the first day of the week and still dark, when Mary of Magdala
came to the tomb. She saw that the stone had been moved away from the tomb and
came running to Simon Peter and the other disciple, the one Jesus loved. "They have
taken the Lord out of the tomb," she said "and we don't know where they have put
him."
So Peter set out with the other disciples to go to the tomb. They ran together, but the
other disciple, running faster than Peter, reached the tomb first; he bent down and
saw the linen cloths lying on the ground, but did not go in. Simon Peter who was
following now came up, went right into the tomb, saw the linen cloths on the
ground, and also the cloth that had been over his head; this was not with the linen
cloths but rolled up in a place by itself. Then the other disciple who had reached the
tomb first also went in; he saw and he believed. Till this moment they had failed to
understand the teaching of scripture, that he must rise from the dead.
This is the Gospel of the Lord. **Praise to you, Lord Jesus Christ.**

The Homily may follow. Then Turn to page 115 *for the Renewal of Baptismal*
Promises, and then Continue on page 7 *with the Offertory Prayers. The Creed is not*
said.

PRAYER OVER THE GIFTS

Lord,
with Easter joy we offer you this sacrifice
by which your Church is reborn and
    nourished
through Christ our Lord.

In the joy of Easter, Lord, we offer you
this sacrifice by which your Church is
wonderfully reborn and sustained.

Turn to page 14 for the Preface of Easter 1

COMMUNION ANTIPHON

Christ has become our paschal sacrifice;
let us feast with the unleavened bread of
sincerity and truth, alleluia.

Christ, our Paschal Lamb, has been
sacrificed.
Let us then, celebrate this festival
with the unleavened bread of sincerity and
truth, alleluia.

PRAYER AFTER COMMUNION

Father of love,
watch over your Church
and bring us to the glory of the
resurrection
promised by this Easter sacrament.

Guard your Church, Lord, in your
never-failing mercy. May the celebration of Easter be a source of new life
to us, so that we may come to share in
the light of the risen Christ.

Turn to page 25 for the Concluding Rite

2nd Sunday of Easter

As the priest goes to the altar everyone joins in this Entrance Antiphon or a hymn.

Like newborn children you should thirst
for milk, on which your spirit can grow to
strength, alleluia.

Like new-born babes, seek the pure
spiritual milk,
on which you may grow up to salvation,
alleluia.

Turn to page 4

OPENING PRAYER

God of mercy,
you wash away our sins in water,
you give us new birth in the Spirit,
and redeem us in the blood of Christ.
As we celebrate Christ's resurrection
increase our awareness of these
blessings,
and renew your gift of life within us.

O God of unfailing mercy, each year at
Easter you rekindle the faith of your
people. Increase the grace you have
given us, and grant us a true
understanding of the baptism which
purified us, the Spirit who gave us new
life, and the Blood which redeemed us.

FIRST READING · Acts 5:12-16

The numbers of men and women who came to believe in the Lord increased steadily.

The faithful all used to meet by common consent in the Portico of Solomon. No one
else ever dared to join them, but the people were loud in their praise and the numbers
of men and women who came to believe in the Lord increased steadily. So many
signs and wonders were worked among the people at the hands of the apostles that
the sick were even taken out into the streets and laid on beds and sleeping-mats in
the hope that at least the shadow of Peter might fall across some of them as he went
past. People even came crowding in from the towns round about Jerusalem,
bringing with them their sick and those tormented by unclean spirits, and all of them
were cured.
This is the word of the Lord. **Thanks be to God.**

RESPONSORIAL PSALM   *Psalm 117:2-4, 22-27*

Give thanks to the Lord for he is good, for his love has no end.

1. Let the sons of Israel say:
"His love has no end."
Let the sons of Aaron say:
"His love has no end."
Let those who fear the Lord say:
"His love has no end."

2. The stone which the builders rejected
has become the corner stone.
This is the work of the Lord,
a marvel in our eyes.
This day was made by the Lord;
we rejoice and are glad.

3. O Lord, grant us salvation;
O Lord, grant success.
Blessed in the name of the Lord
is he who comes.
We bless you from the house of the Lord;
the Lord God is our light.

SECOND READING   *Apocalypse 1:9-13, 17-19*

I was dead and now I am to live for ever and ever.

My name is John, and through our union in Jesus I am your brother and share your sufferings, your kingdom, and all you endure. I was on the island of Patmos for having preached God's word and witnessed for Jesus; it was the Lord's day and the Spirit possessed me, and I heard a voice behind me, shouting like a trumpet, "Write down all that you see in a book." I turned round to see who had spoken to me, and when I turned I saw seven golden lampstands and, surrounded by them, a figure like a Son of man, dressed in a long robe tied at the waist with a golden girdle. When I saw him, I fell in a dead faint at his feet, but he touched me with his right hand and said, "Do not be afraid; it is I, the First and the Last; I am the Living One. I was dead and now I am to live for ever and ever, and I hold the keys of death and of the underworld. Now write down all that you see of present happenings and things that are still to come."

This is the word of the Lord. **Thanks be to God.**

All stand to greet the Gospel. If this Acclamation is not sung it may be omitted.
Alleluia, alleluia! Jesus said: "You believe because you can see me. Happy are those who have not seen and yet believe." Alleluia!

THE GOSPEL   *John 20:19-31*

The Lord be with you. **And also with you.**

A reading from the holy Gospel according to John. **Glory to you, Lord.**

Eight days later, Jesus came.

In the evening of that same day, the first day of the week, the doors were closed in the room where the disciples were, for fear of the Jews. Jesus came and stood among them. He said to them, "Peace be with you," and showed them his hands and his side. The disciples were filled with joy when they saw the Lord, and he said to them again, "Peace be with you. As the Father sent me, so am I sending you." After saying this he breathed on them and said: "Receive the Holy Spirit. For those whose sins you forgive, they are forgiven; for those whose sins you retain, they are retained."

Thomas, called the Twin, who was one of the Twelve, was not with them when Jesus came. When the disciples said, "We have seen the Lord," he answered, "Unless I see the holes that the nails made in his hands and can put my finger into the holes they made, and unless I can put my hand into his side, I refuse to believe." Eight days later the disciples were in the house again and Thomas was with them. The doors were closed, but Jesus came in and stood among them. "Peace be with you" he said. Then he spoke to Thomas, "Put your finger here; look, here are my hands. Give me your hand; put it into my side. Doubt no longer but believe." Thomas replied, "My Lord and my God!" Jesus said to him: "You believe because you can see me. Happy are those who have not seen and yet believe."

There were many other signs that Jesus worked and the disciples saw, but they are not recorded in this book. These are recorded so that you may believe that Jesus is the Christ, the Son of God, and that believing this you may have life through his name.

This is the Gospel of the Lord. **Praise to you, Lord Jesus Christ.**

The Homily may follow, then Turn to page 6 for the Creed.

PRAYER OVER THE GIFTS

Lord,
through faith and baptism
we have become a new creation.
Accept the offering of your people
(and of those born again in baptism)
and bring us to eternal happiness.

Accept, Lord, these offerings your people make to you. When we were baptised and professed our faith in you, we were born to a new life. Grant that we may attain to everlasting happiness in heaven.

Turn to page 14 for the Easter Prefaces

COMMUNION ANTIPHON

Jesus spoke to Thomas: Put your hand here, and see the place of the nails. Doubt no longer, but believe, alleluia.

Put your hand here and feel the print of the nails and do not be faithless but believe, alleluia.

PRAYER AFTER COMMUNION

Almighty God,
may the Easter sacraments we have received
live for ever in our minds and hearts.

Grant us, almighty God, that our souls may always retain the grace of this sacrament of your Son's death and resurrection.

Turn to page 25 for the Concluding Rite

3rd Sunday of Easter

As the priest goes to the altar everyone joins in this Entrance Antiphon or a hymn.

Let all the earth cry out to God with joy; praise the glory of his name; proclaim his glorious praise, alleluia!

Let all the earth praise the Lord, glorifying him and singing hymns in his honour, alleluia.

Turn to page 4

OPENING PRAYER

God our Father,
may we look forward with hope to our resurrection,
for you have made us your sons and daughters,
and restored the joy of our youth.

May we always rejoice, Lord, in the renewal of the youthful vigour of our souls. You have restored to us, our joy and glory as your adopted sons and daughters: may we look forward to the day of our resurrection, in the hope of unfailing happiness.

FIRST READING
Acts 5:27-32, 40-41

We are witnesses of all this, we and the Holy Spirit.

The high priest demanded an explanation of the apostles. "We gave you a formal warning," he said "not to preach in this name, and what have you done? You have filled Jerusalem with your teaching, and seem determined to fix the guilt of this man's death on us." In reply Peter and the apostles said, "Obedience to God comes before obedience to men; it was the God of our ancestors who raised up Jesus, but it was you who had him executed by hanging on a tree. By his own right hand God has now raised him up to be leader and saviour, to give repentance and forgiveness of sins through him to Israel. We are witnesses to all this, we and the Holy Spirit whom God has given to those who obey him." They warned the apostles not to speak in the name of Jesus and released them. And so they left the presence of the Sanhedrin glad to have had the honour of suffering humiliation for the sake of the name.
This is the word of the Lord. **Thanks be to God.**

RESPONSORIAL PSALM
Psalm 29

I will praise you, Lord, you have rescued me.

1. I will praise you, Lord, you have rescued me
and have not let my enemies rejoice over me.
O Lord, you have raised my soul from the dead,
restored me to life from those who sink into the grave.

2. Sing psalms to the Lord, you who love him,
give thanks to his holy name.
His anger lasts but a moment; his favour through life.
At night there are tears, but joy comes with dawn.

3. The Lord listened and had pity.
The Lord came to my help.
For me you have changed my mourning into dancing,
O Lord my God, I will thank you for ever.

SECOND READING
Apocalypse 5:11-14

The Lamb that was sacrificed is worthy to be given riches and power.

In my vision, I, John, heard the sound of an immense number of angels gathered round the throne and the animals and the elders; there were ten thousand times ten thousand of them and thousands upon thousands shouting, "The Lamb that was sacrificed is worthy to be given power, riches, wisdom, strength, honour, glory and blessing." Then I heard all the living things in creation—everything that lives in the air, and on the ground, and under the ground, and in the sea, crying, "To the One who is sitting on the throne and to the Lamb, be all praise, honour, glory and power,

for ever and ever." And the four animals said, "Amen"; and the elders prostrated themselves to worship.
This is the word of the Lord. **Thanks be to God.**
All stand to greet the Gospel. If this Acclamation is not sung it may be omitted.
Alleluia, alleluia! Lord Jesus, explain the scriptures to us. Make our hearts burn within us as you talk to us. Alleluia!

THE GOSPEL   *John 21:1-19*
The Lord be with you. **And also with you.**
A reading from the holy Gospel according to John. **Glory to you, Lord.**
Jesus showed himself again to the disciples. It was by the Sea of Tiberias, and it happened like this: Simon Peter, Thomas called the Twin, Nathanael from Cana in Galilee, the sons of Zebedee and two more of his disciples were together. Simon Peter said, "I'm going fishing." They replied, "We'll come with you." They went out and got into the boat but caught nothing that night.
It was light by now and there stood Jesus on the shore, though the disciples did not realise that it was Jesus. Jesus called out, "Have you caught anything, friends?" And when they answered, "No", he said, "Throw the net out to starboard and you'll find something." So they dropped the net, and there were so many fish that they could not haul it in. The disciple Jesus loved said to Peter, "It is the Lord." At these words "It is the Lord", Simon Peter, who had practically nothing on, wrapped his cloak round him and jumped into the water. The other disciples came on in the boat, towing the net and the fish; they were only about a hundred yards from land.
As soon as they came ashore they saw that there was some bread there, and a charcoal fire with fish cooking on it. Jesus said, "Bring some of the fish you have just caught." Simon Peter went aboard and dragged the net to the shore, full of big fish, one hundred and fifty-three of them; and in spite of there being so many the net was not broken. Jesus said to them, "Come and have breakfast." None of the disciples was bold enough to ask, "Who are you?"; they knew quite well it was the Lord. Jesus then stepped forward, took the bread and gave it to them, and the same with the fish. This was the third time that Jesus showed himself to the disciples after rising from the dead.
After the meal Jesus said to Simon Peter, "Simon son of John, do you love me more than these others do?" He answered, "Yes Lord, you know I love you." Jesus said to him, "Feed my lambs." A second time he said to him, "Simon son of John, do you love me?" He replied, "Yes, Lord, you know I love you." Jesus said to him, "Look after my sheep." Then he said to him a third time, "Simon son of John, do you love me?" Peter was upset that he asked him the third time, "Do you love me?" and said, "Lord, you know everything; you know I love you." Jesus said to him, "Feed my sheep. I tell you most solemnly, when you were young you put on your own belt and walked where you liked; but when you grow old you will stretch out your hands, and somebody else will put a belt round you and take you where you would rather not go." In these words he indicated the kind of death by which Peter would give glory to God. After this he said, "Follow me."
This is the Gospel of the Lord. **Praise to you, Lord Jesus Christ.**

The Homily may follow, then Turn to page 6 for the Creed.

PRAYER OVER THE GIFTS

Lord,
receive these gifts from your Church.
May the great joy you give us
come to perfection in heaven.

Accept, Lord, the gifts your Church offers to you in her rejoicing, and grant that the great joy you have given us may be crowned with eternal happiness in heaven.

Turn to page 14 for the Easter Prefaces

COMMUNION ANTIPHON

Jesus said to his disciples: Come and eat. And he took the bread, and gave it to them, alleluia.

Jesus said to his disciples, Come and eat; and he took the bread and gave it to them, alleluia.

PRAYER AFTER COMMUNION

Lord,
look on your people with kindness
and by these Easter mysteries
bring us to the glory of the resurrection.

In your goodness, Lord, you have nourished your people with the bread of eternal life. Grant that at the Last Day our bodies may rise again in glory with a life that knows no decay.

Turn to page 25 for the Concluding Rite

4th Sunday of Easter

As the priest goes to the altar everyone joins in this Entrance Antiphon or a hymn.

The earth is full of the goodness of the Lord; by the word of the Lord the heavens were made, alleluia.

The earth is full of the mercy of the Lord: by his word the heavens were made, alleluia.

Turn to page 4

OPENING PRAYER

Almighty and ever-living God,
give us new strength
from the courage of Christ our
  shepherd,
and lead us to join the saints in heaven,
where he lives and reigns with you and
  the Holy Spirit,
one God, for ever and ever.

Almighty, eternal God, lead us safely to a share in the joys of heaven. The Good Shepherd courageously opened the way; may we, his flock, humbly follow him there.

FIRST READING

Acts 13:14, 43-52

We must turn to the pagans.

Paul and Barnabas carried on from Perga till they reached Antioch in Pisidia. Here they went to synagogue on the sabbath and took their seats.

When the meeting broke up, many Jews and devout converts joined Paul and Barnabas, and in their talks with them Paul and Barnabas urged them to remain faithful to the grace God had given them.

The next sabbath almost the entire town assembled to hear the word of God. When they saw the crowds, the Jews, prompted by jealousy, used blasphemies and contradicted everything Paul said. Then Paul and Barnabas spoke out boldly. "We had to proclaim the word of God to you first, but since you have rejected it, since you do not think yourselves worthy of eternal life, we must turn to the pagans. For this is what the Lord commanded us to do when he said: I have made you a light for the nations, so that my salvation may reach the ends of the earth."

It made the pagans very happy to hear this and they thanked the Lord for his message; all who were destined for eternal life became believers. Thus the word of the Lord spread through the whole countryside.

But the Jews worked upon some of the devout women of the upper classes and the leading men of the city and persuaded them to turn against Paul and Barnabas and expel them from their territory. So they shook the dust from their feet in defiance and went off to Iconium; but the disciples were filled with joy and the Holy Spirit. This is the word of the Lord. **Thanks be to God.**

RESPONSORIAL PSALM
Psalm 99

We are his people, the sheep of his flock.

1. Cry out with joy to the Lord, all the earth.
Serve the Lord with gladness.
Come before him, singing for joy.

2. Know that he, the Lord, is God.
He made us, we belong to him,
we are his people, the sheep of his flock.

3. Indeed, how good is the Lord,
eternal his merciful love.
He is faithful from age to age.

SECOND READING
Apocalypse 7:9, 14-17

The Lamb will be their shepherd and will lead them to springs of living water.

I, John, saw a huge number, impossible to count, of people from every nation, race, tribe and language; they were standing in front of the throne and in front of the Lamb, dressed in white robes and holding palms in their hands. One of the elders said to me, "These are the people who have been through the great persecution, and because they have washed their robes white again in the blood of the Lamb, they now stand in front of God's throne and serve him day and night in his sanctuary; and the One who sits on the throne will spread his tent over them. They will never hunger or thirst again; neither the sun nor scorching wind will ever plague them, because the Lamb who is at the throne will be their shepherd and will lead them to springs of living water; and God will wipe away all tears from their eyes." This is the word of the Lord. **Thanks be to God.**

All stand to greet the Gospel. If this Acclamation is not sung it may be omitted.
Alleluia, alleluia! I am the good shepherd, says the Lord; I know my own sheep and my own know me. Alleluia!

THE GOSPEL
John 10:27-30

The Lord be with you. **And also with you.**
A reading from the holy Gospel according to John. **Glory to you, Lord.**
I give eternal life to the sheep that belong to me.
Jesus said: "The sheep that belong to me listen to my voice; I know them and they follow me. I give them eternal life; they will never be lost and no one will ever steal

them from me. The Father who gave them to me is greater than anyone and no one can steal from the Father. The Father and I are one." This is the Gospel of the Lord. **Praise to you, Lord Jesus Christ.**

The Homily may follow, then Turn to page 6 for the Creed.

PRAYER OVER THE GIFTS

Lord,
restore us by these Easter mysteries.
May the continuing work of our Redeemer
bring us eternal joy.

Grant, Lord, that we may always find joy in this sacrament of your Son's death and resurrection, so that the grace of our redemption may ever be at work in our souls to bring us to the everlasting joy of heaven.

Turn to page 14 for the Easter Prefaces

COMMUNION ANTIPHON

The Good Shepherd is risen! He who laid down his life for his sheep, who died for his flock, he is risen, alleluia.

The Good Shepherd, who laid down his life for his sheep and in his love died for his flock, has risen from the dead, alleluia.

PRAYER AFTER COMMUNION

Father, eternal shepherd,
watch over the flock redeemed by the blood of Christ
and lead us to the promised land.

Heavenly Father, you are our Shepherd. Look with mercy upon the sheep of your flock which you redeemed with your Son's precious blood, and lead them to your pastures in heaven.

Turn to page 25 for the Concluding Rite

5th Sunday of Easter

As the priest goes to the altar everyone joins in this Entrance Antiphon or a hymn.

Sing to the Lord a new song, for he has done marvellous deeds; he has revealed to the nations his saving power, alleluia.

**Sing to the Lord a new song, for he has done marvellous deeds.
He has revealed his mercy and justice be before the eyes of all peoples, alleluia.**

Turn to page 4

OPENING PRAYER

God our Father,
look upon us with love.
You redeem us and make us your children in Christ.
Give us true freedom
and bring us the inheritance you promised.

You have redeemed us, O God, and adopted us as your children. Look kindly upon your beloved sons and daughters who believe in Christ, and grant them true freedom and their eternal inheritance.

FIRST READING   *Acts 14:21-27*
They gave an account to the church of all that God had done with them.
Paul and Barnabas went back through Lystra and Iconium to Antioch. They put
fresh heart into the disciples, encouraging them to persevere in the faith. "We all
have to experience many hardships" they said "before we enter the kingdom of
God." In each of these churches they appointed elders, and with prayer and fasting
they commended them to the Lord in whom they had come to believe.
They passed through Pisidia and reached Pamphylia. Then after proclaiming the
word at Perga they went down to Attalia and from there sailed for Antioch, where
they had originally been commended to the grace of God for the work they had now
completed.
On their arrival they assembled the church and gave an account of all that God had
done with them, and how he had opened the door of faith to the pagans.
This is the word of the Lord. **Thanks be to God.**

RESPONSORIAL PSALM   *Psalm 144*
I will bless your name for ever, O God my King.
1. The Lord is kind and full of
   compassion,
slow to anger, abounding in love.
How good is the Lord to all,
compassionate to all his creatures.

2. All your creatures shall thank you, O
   Lord,
and your friends shall repeat their
   blessing.
They shall speak of the glory of your reign
and declare your might, O God,
to make known to men your mighty deeds
and the glorious splendour of your reign.

3. Yours is an everlasting kingdom,
   your rule lasts from age to age.

SECOND READING   *Apocalypse 21:1-5*
God will wipe away all tears from their eyes.
I, John, saw a new heaven and a new earth; the first heaven and the first earth had
disappeared now, and there was no longer any sea. I saw the holy city, and the new
Jerusalem, coming down from God out of heaven, as beautiful as a bride all dressed
for her husband. Then I heard a loud voice call from the throne, "You see this city?
Here God lives among men. He will make his home among them; they shall be his
people, and he will be their God; his name is God-with-them. He will wipe away all
tears from their eyes; there will be no more death, and no more mourning or
sadness. The world of the past has gone."
Then the One sitting on the throne spoke: "Now I am making the whole of creation
new" he said.
This is the word of the Lord. **Thanks be to God.**
All stand to greet the Gospel. If this Acclamation is not sung it may be omitted.
**Alleluia, alleluia! Jesus said: "I give you a new commandment: love one another, just
as I have loved you." Alleluia!**

THE GOSPEL   *John 13:31-35*
The Lord be with you. **And also with you.**
A reading from the holy Gospel according to John. **Glory to you, Lord.**
I give you a new commandment: love one another.
When Judas had gone Jesus said: "Now has the Son of Man been glorified, and in
him God has been glorified. If God has been glorified in him, God will in turn glorify
him in himself, and will glorify him very soon. My little children, I shall not be with
you much longer. I give you a new commandment: love one another; just as I have
loved you, you also must love one another. By this love you have for one another,
every one will know that you are my disciples."
This is the Gospel of the Lord. **Praise to you, Lord Jesus Christ.**

The Homily may follow, then | *Turn to page 6 for the Creed.* |

PRAYER OVER THE GIFTS

Lord God,
by this holy exchange of gifts
you share with us your divine life.
Grant that everything we do
may be directed by the knowledge of
    your truth.

Through this holy sacrifice, Lord, you
have enabled us to share in your own
divine life. You have taught us your
truth: grant us the grace to live by it.

| *Turn to page 14 for the Easter Prefaces* |

COMMUNION ANTIPHON
**I am the vine and you are the branches,
says the Lord; he who lives in me, and I in
him, will bear much fruit, alleluia.**

**I am the true vine; you are the branches,
    says the Lord.
He who abides in me, and I in him,
he it is that bears much fruit, alleluia.**

PRAYER AFTER COMMUNION
Merciful Father,
may these mysteries give us new purpose
and bring us to a new life in you.

You have nourished your people, Lord,
with the Bread of Heaven: in your
goodness grant us the grace to turn from
our old ways to a new life.

| *Turn to page 25 for the Concluding Rite* |

6th Sunday of Easter

As the priest goes to the altar everyone joins in this Entrance Antiphon or a hymn.
**Speak out with a voice of joy; let it be
heard to the ends of the earth: The Lord
has set his people free, alleluia.**

**Proclaim the good news to the ends of the
    earth so that all may hear it:
the Lord has set his people free, alleluia.**

| *Turn to page 4* |

OPENING PRAYER

Ever-living God,
help us to celebrate our joy
in the resurrection of the Lord
and to express in our lives
the love we celebrate.

Almighty God, give us lasting gladness
in celebrating this joyful season when we
honour our risen Lord. Grant that our
annual commemoration of the resurrection may bear fruit in our lives.

FIRST READING
Acts 15:1-2, 22-29

It has been decided by the Holy Spirit and by ourselves not to saddle you with any burden beyond these essentials.

Some men came down from Judaea and taught the brothers, "Unless you have yourselves circumcised in the tradition of Moses you cannot be saved." This led to disagreement, and after Paul and Barnabas had had a long argument with these men it was arranged that Paul and Barnabas and others of the church should go up to Jerusalem and discuss the problem with the apostles and elders.

Then the apostles and elders decided to choose delegates to send to Antioch with Paul and Barnabas; the whole church concurred with this. They chose Judas known as Barsabbas and Silas, both leading men in the brotherhood, and gave them this letter to take with them:

"The apostles and elders, your brothers, send greetings to the brothers of pagan birth in Antioch, Syria and Cilicia. We hear that some of our members have disturbed you with their demands and have unsettled your minds. They acted without any authority from us, and so we have decided unanimously to elect delegates and to send them to you with Barnabas and Paul, men we highly respect who have dedicated their lives to the name of our Lord Jesus Christ. Accordingly we are sending you Judas and Silas, who will confirm by word of mouth what we have written in this letter. It has been decided by the Holy Spirit and by ourselves not to saddle you with any burden beyond these essentials: you are to abstain from food sacrificed to idols, from blood, from the meat of strangled animals and from fornication. Avoid these, and you will do what is right. Farewell."

This is the word of the Lord. **Thanks be to God.**

RESPONSORIAL PSALM
Psalm 66

Let the peoples praise you, O God; let all the peoples praise you.

1. O God, be gracious and bless us
and let your face shed its light upon us.
So will your ways be known upon earth
and all nations learn your saving help.

2. Let the nations be glad and exult
for you rule the world with justice.
With fairness you rule the peoples,
you guide the nations on earth.

3. Let the peoples praise you, O God;
let all the peoples praise you.
May God still give us his blessing
till the ends of the earth revere him.

SECOND READING
Apocalypse 21: 10-14, 22-23

He showed me the holy city coming down out of heaven.

In the spirit, the angel took me to the top of an enormous high mountain and showed me Jerusalem, the holy city, coming down from God out of heaven. It had all the radiant glory of God and glittered like some precious jewel of crystal-clear diamond. The walls of it were of a great height, and had twelve gates; at each of the twelve gates there was an angel, and over the gates were written the names of the twelve tribes of Israel; on the east there were three gates, on the north three gates, on the south three gates, and on the west three gates. The city walls stood on twelve foundation stones, each one of which bore the name of one of the twelve apostles of the Lamb.

I saw that there was no temple in the city since the Lord God Almighty and the Lamb were themselves the temple, and the city did not need the sun or the moon for light, since it was lit by the radiant glory of God and the Lamb was a lighted torch for it.

This is the word of the Lord. **Thanks be to God.**

All stand to greet the Gospel. If this Acclamation is not sung it may be omitted.
Alleluia, alleluia! Jesus said: "If anyone loves me he will keep my word, and my Father will love him, and we shall come to him. Alleluia!

THE GOSPEL   *John 14:23-29*

The Lord be with you. **And also with you.**
A reading from the holy Gospel according to John. **Glory to you, Lord.**
The Holy Spirit will remind you of all I have said to you.

Jesus said to his disciples: "If anyone loves me he will keep my word, and my Father will love him, and we shall come to him and make our home with him. Those who do not love me do not keep my words. And my word is not my own: it is the word of the one who sent me. I have said these things to you while still with you; but the Advocate, the Holy Spirit, whom the Father will send in my name, will teach you everything and remind you of all I have said to you. Peace I bequeath to you, my own peace I give you, a peace the world cannot give, this is my gift to you. Do not let your hearts be troubled or afraid. You heard me say: I am going away, and shall return. If you loved me you would have been glad to know that I am going to the Father, for the Father is greater than I. I have told you this now before it happens, so that when it does happen you may believe."

This is the Gospel of the Lord. **Praise to you, Lord Jesus Christ.**

The Homily may follow, then *Turn to page 6 for the Creed.*

PRAYER OVER THE GIFTS

Lord,
accept our prayers and offerings.
Make us worthy of your sacraments of
love
by granting us your forgiveness.

You have called us, Lord, to be your followers and washed away our sins. Accept our prayers and offerings, and make us worthy to receive the sacrament of your love.

Turn to page 14 for the Easter Prefaces

COMMUNION ANTIPHON

If you love me, keep my commandments, says the Lord. The Father will send you the Holy Spirit, to be with you for ever, alleluia.

**If you love me, keep my commandments, says the Lord.
I will ask the Father and he will give you another Comforter
to be with you for ever, alleluia.**

PRAYER AFTER COMMUNION

Almighty and ever-living Lord,
you restored us to life
by raising Christ from death.
Strengthen us by this Easter sacrament;
may we feel its saving power in our daily
life.

Almighty, eternal God, through your
Son's resurrection you restore us to
eternal life; you have given us his risen
Body and Blood to be the food for our
souls. Grant that the grace of this
sacrament may grow within us and
strengthen our hearts.

Turn to page 25 for the Concluding Rite

Ascension

As the priest goes to the altar everyone joins in this Entrance Antiphon or a hymn.

**Men of Galilee, why do you stand looking
in the sky? The Lord will return, just as
you have seen him ascend, alleluia.**

**Men of Galilee, why do you stand in
wonder gazing up to heaven?
He will come again in the same way as
you saw him ascending
to heaven, alleluia.**

Turn to page 4

OPENING PRAYER

God our Father,
make us joyful in the ascension of your
Son Jesus Christ.
May we follow him into the new
creation,
for his ascension is our glory and our
hope.

Almighty God, fill our hearts with joy
and gratitude at your Son's ascension,
which is our triumph; for as our Head
has gone before, we, the members of his
Body, hope to follow him into glory.

FIRST READING   *Acts 1:1-11*

He was lifted up while they looked on.

In my earlier work, Theophilus, I dealt with everything Jesus had done and taught
from the beginning until the day he gave his instructions to the apostles he had
chosen through the Holy Spirit, and was taken up to heaven. He had shown himself
alive to them after his Passion by many demonstrations: for forty days he had
continued to appear to them and tell them about the kingdom of God. When he had
been at table with them, he had told them not to leave Jerusalem, but to wait there
for what the Father had promised. "It is," he had said, "what you have heard me
speak about: John baptised with water but you, not many days from now, will be
baptised with the Holy Spirit."
Now having met together, they asked him, "Lord, has the time come? Are you going
to restore the kingdom to Israel?" He replied, "It is not for you to know times or
dates that the Father has decided by his own authority, but you will receive power
when the Holy Spirit comes on you, and then you will be my witnesses not only in
Jerusalem but throughout Judaea and Samaria, and indeed to the ends of the
earth."
As he said this he was lifted up while they looked on, and a cloud took him from

their sight. They were still staring into the sky when suddenly two men in white were standing near them and they said, "Why are you men from Galilee standing here looking into the sky? Jesus who has been taken up from you into heaven, this same Jesus will come back in the same way as you have seen him go there." This is the word of the Lord. **Thanks be to God.**

RESPONSORIAL PSALM   *Psalm 46*

God goes up with shouts of joy: the Lord goes up with trumpet blast.

1. All peoples, clap your hands,
cry to God with shouts of joy!
For the Lord, the Most High, we must
    fear,
great king over all the earth.

2. God goes up with shouts of joy;
the Lord goes up with trumpet blast.
Sing praise for God, sing praise,
sing praise to our king, sing praise.

3. God is king of all the earth.
Sing praise with all your skill.
God is king over the nations;
God reigns on his holy throne.

SECOND READING   *Ephesians 1:17-23*

He made him sit at his right hand in heaven.

May the God of our Lord Jesus Christ, the Father of glory, give you a spirit of wisdom and perception of what is revealed, to bring you to full knowledge of him. May he enlighten the eyes of your mind so that you can see what hope his call holds for you, what rich glories he has promised the saints will inherit and how infinitely great is the power that he has exercised for us believers. This you can tell from the strength of his power at work in Christ, when he used it to raise him from the dead and to make him sit at his right hand, in heaven, far above every Sovereignty, Authority, Power, or Domination, or any other name that can be named, not only in this age, but also in the age to come. He has put all things under his feet, and made him, as the ruler of everything, the head of the Church; which is his body, the fullness of him who fills the whole creation. This is the word of the Lord. **Thanks be to God.**

All stand to greet the Gospel. If this Acclamation is not sung it may be omitted.

Alleluia, alleluia! Go, make disciples of all the nations; I am with you always; yes, to the end of time. Alleluia!

THE GOSPEL   *Luke 24:46-53*

The Lord be with you. **And also with you.**

A reading from the holy Gospel according to Luke. **Glory to you, Lord.**

As he blessed them he was carried up to heaven.

Jesus said to his disciples: "You see how it is written that the Christ would suffer and on the third day rise from the dead, and that, in his name, repentance for the forgiveness of sins would be preached to all the nations, beginning from Jerusalem. You are witnesses to this.

"And now I am sending down to you what the Father has promised. Stay in the city then, until you are clothed with the power from on high."

Then he took them out as far as the outskirts of Bethany, and lifting up his hands he blessed them. Now as he blessed them, he withdrew from them and was carried up to

heaven. They worshipped him and then went back to Jerusalem full of joy; and they were continually in the Temple praising God.
This is the Gospel of the Lord. **Praise to you, Lord Jesus Christ.**

The Homily may follow, then ⌈*Turn to page 6 for the Creed.*⌉

PRAYER OVER THE GIFTS

Lord,
receive our offering
as we celebrate the ascension of Christ
  your Son.
May his gifts help us rise with him
to the joys of heaven,
where he lives and reigns for ever and
  ever.

Lord, we offer you this sacrifice in gratitude for your Son's glorious ascension. Grant that it may help us to lift up our hearts with him from the things of this world to those of heaven.

⌈*Turn to page 8 for the Preface*⌉

COMMUNION ANTIPHON

I, the Lord, am with you always, until the end of the world, alleluia.

You will see, I am with you always, to the end of the world, alleluia.

PRAYER AFTER COMMUNION

Father,
in this eucharist
we touch the divine life you give to the
  world.
Help us to follow Christ with love
to eternal life where he is Lord for ever
  and ever.

Almighty, eternal God, you allow us to share in the gifts of heaven while we are still on earth. Grant that our hearts may always rise up to you, for in you our humanity is glorified.

⌈*Turn to page 25 for the Concluding Rite*⌉

7th Sunday of Easter

As the priest goes to the altar everyone joins in this Entrance Antiphon or a hymn.

Lord, hear my voice when I call to you. My heart has prompted me to seek your face; I seek it, Lord; do not hide from me, alleluia.

⌈*Turn to page 4*⌉

Lord, hear my voice when I call to you; my heart has spoken to you. I have sought your face and I shall seek it again. Do not turn your eyes away from me, alleluia.

OPENING PRAYER

Father,
help us keep in mind that Christ our
  Saviour
lives with you in glory
and promised to remain with us until the
  end of time.

We believe, Lord, that the Saviour of mankind is with you in your glory. Grant that we also may experience his abiding presence among us, as he promised, to the end of the world.

FIRST READING　　　　　　　　　　　　　　　　　　　*Acts 7:55-60*

I can see the Son of Man standing at the right hand of God.

Stephen, filled with the Holy Spirit, gazed into heaven and saw the glory of God, and Jesus standing at God's right hand. "I can see heaven thrown open" he said "and the Son of Man standing at the right hand of God." At this all the members of the council shouted out and stopped their ears with their hands; then they all rushed at him, sent him out of the city and stoned him. The witnesses put down their clothes at the feet of a young man called Saul. As they were stoning him, Stephen said in invocation, "Lord Jesus, receive my spirit." Then he knelt down and said aloud, "Lord, do not hold this sin against them"; and with these words he fell asleep. This is the word of the Lord. **Thanks be to God.**

RESPONSORIAL PSALM　　　　　　　　　　　　　　　　*Psalm 96*

The Lord is king, most high above all the earth.

1. The Lord is king, let earth rejoice,　2. The skies proclaim his justice;
the many coastlands be glad.　　　　　　all peoples see his glory.
His throne is justice and right.　　　　　All you spirits, worship him.

3. For you indeed are the Lord
most high above all the earth
exalted far above all spirits.

SECOND READING　　　　　　　　　*Apocalypse 22:12-14, 16-17, 20*

Come, Lord Jesus.

I, John, heard a voice speaking to me: "Very soon now, I shall be with you again, bringing the reward to be given to every man according to what he deserves. I am the Alpha and the Omega, the First and the Last, the Beginning and the End. Happy are those who will have washed their robes clean, so that they will have the right to feed on the tree of life and can come through the gates into the city."

I, Jesus, have sent my angel to make these revelations to you for the sake of the churches. I am of David's line, the root of David and the bright star of the morning. The Spirit and the Bride say, "Come." Let everyone who listens answer, "Come." Then let all who are thirsty come; all who want it may have the water of life, and have it free.

The one who guarantees these revelations repeats his promise: I shall indeed be with you. Amen; come, Lord Jesus.

This is the word of the Lord. **Thanks be to God.**

All stand to greet the Gospel. If this Acclamation is not sung it may be omitted.
Alleluia, alleluia! I will not leave you orphans, says the Lord; I will come back to you, and your hearts will be full of joy. Alleluia.

THE GOSPEL　　　　　　　　　　　　　　　　　　　*John 17:20-26*

The Lord be with you. **And also with you.**

A reading from the holy Gospel according to John. **Glory to you, Lord.**

May they be completely one.

Jesus raised his eyes to heaven and said: "Holy Father, I pray not only for these, but for those also who through their words will believe in me. May they all be one. Father, may they be one in us, as you are in me and I am in you, so that the world may believe it was you who sent me. I have given them the glory you gave to me, that they may be one as we are one. With me in them and you in me, may they be so completely one that the world will realise that it was you who sent me and that I have loved them as much as you loved me. Father, I want those you have given me to be with me where I am, so that they may always see the glory you have given me because you loved me before the foundation of the world. Father, Righteous One, the world has not known you, but I have known you, and these have known that you have sent me. I have made your name known to them and will continue to make it known, so that the love with which you loved me may be in them, and so that I may be in them."

This is the Gospel of the Lord. **Praise to you, Lord Jesus Christ.**

The Homily may follow, then | *Turn to page 6 for the Creed.*

PRAYER OVER THE GIFTS

Lord,
accept the prayers and gifts
we offer in faith and love.
May this eucharist
bring us to your glory.

Accept, Lord, our prayers and our offerings. Grant that our loving worship may help us to reach the glory of heaven.

Turn to page 8 for the Preface

COMMUNION ANTIPHON

This is the prayer of Jesus: that his believers may become one as he is one with the Father, alleluia.

**I ask you, Father,
that they may be one as we are one,
alleluia.**

PRAYER AFTER COMMUNION

God our Saviour,
hear us,
and through this holy mystery give us hope
that the glory you have given Christ will be given to the Church, his body, for he is Lord for ever and ever.

We ask you, God our Saviour, that this holy sacrament may strengthen us in our hope that the glory which Christ our Head has already attained, will belong also to his whole Body the Church.

Turn to page 25 for the Concluding Rite

DECEMBER 8

Immaculate Conception

As the priest goes to the altar everyone joins in this Entrance Antiphon or a hymn.

I exult for joy in the Lord, my soul rejoices in my God; for he has clothed me in the garment of salvation and robed me in the cloak of justice, like a bride adorned with her jewels.

I will greatly rejoice in the Lord, and my soul will triumph in God; for he has clothed me with holiness and robed me with grace, like a bride adorned with her bridal dress.

Turn to page 4

OPENING PRAYER

Father,
you prepared the Virgin Mary
to be the worthy mother of your Son.
You let her share beforehand
in the salvation Christ would bring by
  his death,
and kept her sinless from the first
  moment of her conception.
Help us by her prayers to live
in your presence without sin.

O God, you prepared a worthy dwelling-place for your Son through the Immaculate Conception of the Virgin Mary and preserved her from all taint of sin through the merits of his future death. Grant through her intercession that we too may be freed from sin and join your company in heaven.

FIRST READING
Genesis 3:9-15, 20

I will make you enemies of each other: your offspring and her offspring.

After Adam had eaten of the tree, the Lord God called to him. "Where are you?" he asked. "I heard the sound of you in the garden," he replied. "I was afraid because I was naked, so I hid." "Who told you that you were naked?" he asked. "Have you been eating of the tree I forbade you to eat?" The man replied, "It was the woman you put with me; she gave me the fruit, and I ate it." Then the Lord God asked the woman, "What is this you have done?" The woman replied, "The serpent tempted me and I ate."
Then the Lord God said to the serpent, "Because you have done this, be accursed beyond all cattle, all wild beasts. You shall crawl on your belly and eat dust every day of your life. I will make you enemies of each other: you and the woman, your offspring and her offspring. It will crush your head and you will strike its heel."
The man named his wife "Eve because she was the mother of all those who live".
This is the word of the Lord. **Thanks be to God.**

RESPONSORIAL PSALM
Psalm 79

Sing a new song to the Lord for he has worked wonders.

1. Sing a new song to the Lord
for he has worked wonders.
His right hand and his holy arm
have brought salvation.

2. The Lord has made known his
   salvation;
has shown his justice to the nations.
He has remembered his truth and love
for the house of Israel.

3. All the ends of the earth have seen
the salvation of our God.
Shout to the Lord all the earth,
ring out your joy.

SECOND READING
Ephesians 1:3-6, 11-12

Before the world was made, God chose us in Christ.

Blessed be God the Father of our Lord Jesus Christ, who has blessed us with all the spiritual blessings of heaven in Christ. Before the world was made, he chose us, chose us in Christ, to be holy and spotless, and to live through love in his presence, determining that we should become his adopted sons, through Jesus Christ for his own kind purposes, to make us praise the glory of his grace, his free gift to us in the Beloved. And it is in him that we were claimed as God's own, chosen from the beginning, under the predetermined plan of the one who guides all things as he

decides by his own will; chosen to be, for his greater glory, the people who would put their hopes in Christ before he came.
This is the word of the Lord. **Thanks be to God.**
All stand to greet the Gospel. If this Acclamation is not sung it may be omitted.
Alleluia, alleluia! Hail, Mary, full of grace; the Lord is with thee! Blessed art thou among women. Alleluia!

THE GOSPEL   *Luke 1:26-38*
The Lord be with you. **And also with you.**
A reading from the holy Gospel according to Luke. **Glory to you, Lord.**
Rejoice, so highly favoured! The Lord is with you.
The angel Gabriel was sent by God to a town in Galilee called Nazareth, to a virgin betrothed to a man named Joseph, of the House of David; and the virgin's name was Mary. He went in and said to her, "Rejoice, so highly favoured! The Lord is with you." She was deeply disturbed by these words and asked herself what this greeting could mean, but the angel said to her, "Mary, do not be afraid; you have won God's favour. Listen! You are to conceive and bear a son, and you must name him Jesus. He will be great and will be called Son of the Most High. The Lord God will give him the throne of his ancestor David; he will rule over the House of Jacob for ever and his reign will have no end." Mary said to the angel, "But how can this come about, since I am a virgin?" "The Holy Spirit will come upon you" the angel answered "and the power of the Most High will cover you with its shadow. And so the child will be holy and will be called Son of God. Know this too: your kinswoman Elizabeth has, in her old age, herself conceived a son, and she whom people called barren is now in her sixth month, for nothing is impossible to God." "I am the handmaid of the Lord," said Mary "let what you have said be done to me." And the angel left her.
This is the Gospel of the Lord. **Praise to you, Lord Jesus Christ.**

The Homily may follow, then Turn to page 6 for the Creed.

PRAYER OVER THE GIFTS

Lord,
accept this sacrifice
on the feast of the sinless Virgin Mary.
You kept her free from sin
from the first moment of her life.
Help us by her prayers,
and free us from our sins.

Turn to page 8 for the Preface

We offer you, Lord, this redeeming sacrifice in honour of the Immaculate Conception of the Blessed Virgin Mary. We believe that your grace preserved her in advance from all taint of sin: in your mercy accept our offering, and through her intercession keep us free from all guilt.

COMMUNION ANTIPHON

All honour to you, Mary! From you arose the sun of justice, Christ our God.

O Mary, great is your glory;
from you was born the Sun of Justice,
Christ our God.

PRAYER AFTER COMMUNION

Lord our God,
in your love, you chose the Virgin Mary
and kept her free from sin.
May this sacrament of your love
free us from our sins.

Lord our God, by a unique privilege you
preserved Our Lady from all sin. Grant
that the sacrament we have received
may heal the wounds which sin has
inflicted on us.

Turn to page 25 for the Concluding Rite

Mass for Christian Unity

As the priest goes to the altar everyone joins in this Entrance Antiphon or a hymn.

I am the Good Shepherd. I know my
sheep, and mine know me, says the Lord,
just as the Father knows me and I know
the Father. I gave my life for my sheep.

I am the good Shepherd;
I know my sheep and they know me,
   says the Lord.
As the Father knows me, I know the
   Father,
and I lay down my life for my sheep.

Turn to page 4

OPENING PRAYER

Almighty and eternal God,
you keep together those you have
   united.
Look kindly on all who follow Jesus your
   Son.
We are all consecrated to you by our
   common baptism;
make us one in the fullness of faith
and keep us one in the fellowship of
love.

Almighty, eternal God, those who are
divided you unite, and those who are
united you support. Look with mercy on
your Son's flock. The same baptism has
made us holy; may we all share the same
faith in its fulness, and be linked in a
bond of love.

FIRST READING   *Ezekiel 36:23-28*

I am going to gather you together from all countries, and I shall give you a new heart.

The Lord God says this:
I mean to display the holiness of my great name, which has been profaned among
the nations, which you have profaned among them. And the nations will learn that I
am the Lord—it is the Lord who speaks—when I display my holiness for your sake
before their eyes. Then I am going to take you from among the nations and gather
you together from all the foreign countries, and bring you home to your own land. I
shall pour clean water over you and you will be cleansed; I shall cleanse you of all
your defilement and all your idols. I shall give you a new heart, and put a new spirit
in you; I shall remove the heart of stone from your bodies and give you a heart of
flesh instead. I shall put my spirit in you, and make you keep my laws and sincerely
respect my observances. You will live in the land which I gave your ancestors. You
shall be my people and I shall be your God.
This is the word of the Lord. **Thanks be to God.**

RESPONSORIAL PSALM *Psalm 121*
I rejoiced when I heard them say: Let us go to God's house.

1. I rejoiced when I heard them say:
'Let us go to God's house.'
And now our feet are standing
with your gates, O Jerusalem.

2. Jerusalem is built as a city
strongly compact.
It is there that the tribes go up,
the tribes of the Lord.

3. For Israel's law it is,
there to praise the Lord's name.
There were set the thrones of judgment
of the house of David.

4. For the peace of Jerusalem pray:
'peace be to your homes!
May peace reign in your walls,
in your palaces, peace!'

5. For love of my brethren and friends
I say: 'Peace upon you!'
For love of the house of the Lord
I will ask for your good.

SECOND READING *Ephesians 4:30-5:2*
Forgive each other as readily as God forgave you in Christ.

Do not grieve the Holy Spirit of God who has marked you with his seal for you to be set free when the day comes. Never have grudges against others, or lose your temper, or raise your voice to anybody, or call each other names, or allow any sort of spitefulness. Be friends with one another, and kind, forgiving each other as readily as God forgave you in Christ.
Try, then, to imitate God, as children of his that he loves, and follow Christ by loving as he loved you, giving himself up in our place as a fragrant offering and a sacrifice to God.
This is the word of the Lord. **Thanks be to God.**

All stand to greet the Gospel. If this Acclamation is not sung it may be omitted.
Alleluia, alleluia! Gather your Church together, Lord, from the ends of the earth into your kingdom, for glory and power are yours through Jesus Christ for ever. Alleluia!

THE GOSPEL *John 17:20-26*
The Lord be with you. **And also with you.**
A reading from the holy Gospel according to John. **Glory to you, Lord.**
May they be so completely one.

Jesus raised his eyes to heaven and said: 'Holy Father, I pray not only for these, but for those who through their words will believe in me. May they all be one. Father, may they be one in us, as you are in me and I am in you, so that the world may believe it was you who sent me. I have given them the glory you gave me, that they may be one as we are one. With me in them and you in me, may they be so completely one that the world will realise that it was you who sent me and that I have loved them as much as you loved me. Father, I want those you have given me to be with me where I am, so that they may always see the glory you have given me because you loved me before the foundation of the world. Father, Righteous One, the world has not known you, but I have known you, and these have known that you have sent me. I have made your name known to them and will continue to make it known, so that the love with which you loved me may be in them, and so that I may be in them.'
This is the Gospel of the Lord. **Praise to you, Lord Jesus Christ.**

The Homily may follow, then Turn to page 6 for the Creed.

PRAYER OVER THE GIFTS

Lord,
by one perfect sacrifice
you gained us as your people.
Bless us and all your Church
with gifts of unity and peace.

Lord, by one sacrifice never to be
repeated, you adopted us as your own
people. Grant, then, to your Church the
gifts of unity and peace.

Turn to page 8 for the Preface

COMMUNION ANTIPHON

**Because there is one bread, we, though
many, are one body, for we all share in the
one loaf and in the one cup.**

**Though we are many, we are one bread
and one body,
for we all share the same bread and the
same chalice.**

PRAYER AFTER COMMUNION

Lord,
may this holy communion,
the sign and promise of our unity in you,
make that unity a reality in your
Church.

We have received your Holy Communion, Lord. It is the sign that your
faithful are to be united in you; grant
that it may be the source of unity in your
Church.

Turn to page 25 for the Concluding Rite

Mass for Peace

As the priest goes to the altar everyone joins in this Entrance Antiphon or a hymn.

**Give peace, Lord, to those who wait for
you; listen to the prayers of your servants,
and guide us in the way of justice.**

**Grant peace, Lord, to those who wait
upon your will;
listen to the prayers of your servants.
Direct our footsteps along the paths of
justice.**

Turn to page 4

OPENING PRAYER

God our Father,
you reveal that those who work for
peace
will be called your sons.
Help us to work without ceasing
for that justice
which brings true and lasting peace.

O God, you have taught us that those
who seek peace will be called your
children. Help us to establish continually that justice which is the only
guarantee of true and lasting peace.

FIRST READING   *Isaiah 9:1-6*

Wide is the dominion of the Lord, in a peace that has no end.

The people that walked in darkness has seen a great light; on those who live in a land
of deep shadow a light has shone. You have made their gladness greater, you have
made their joy increase; they rejoice in your presence as men rejoice at harvest time,
as men are happy when they are dividing the spoils. For the yoke that was weighing
on him, the bar across his shoulders, the rod of his oppressor, these you break as on
the day of Midian. For all the footgear of battle, every cloak rolled in blood, is burnt

and consumed by fire. For there is a child born for us, a son given to us and dominion is laid on his shoulders; and this is the name they give him: Wonder-Counsellor, Mighty-God, Eternal-Father, Prince-of-Peace. This is the word of the Lord. **Thanks be to God.**

RESPONSORIAL PSALM   *Psalm 71*

In his days justice shall flourish and peace till the moon fails.

1. O God, give your judgment to the King,
to a king's son your justice,
that he may judge your people in justice
and your poor in right judgment.

2. May the mountains bring forth peace for the people
and the hills, justice.
May he defend the poor of the people
and save the children of the needy.

3. In his days justice shall flourish
and peace till the moon fails.
He shall rule from sea to sea,
from the Great River to earth's bounds.

4. For he shall save the poor when they cry
and the needy who are helpless.
He will have pity on the weak
and save the lives of the poor.

5. May his name be blessed for ever
and endure like the sun.
Every tribe shall be blessed in him,
all nations bless his name.

SECOND READING   *James 3:13-18*

The harvest of justice is sown in peace by those who make peace.

If there are any wise or learned men among you, let them show it by their good lives, with humility and wisdom in their actions. But if at heart you have the bitterness of jealously, or a self-seeking ambition, never make any claims for yourself or cover up the truth with lies—principles of this kind are not the wisdom that comes down from above: they are only earthly, animal and devilish. Wherever you find jealously and ambition, you find disharmony, and wicked things of every kind being done; whereas the wisdom that comes down from above is essentially something pure; it also makes for peace, and is kindly and considerate; it is full of compassion and shows itself by doing good; nor is there any trace of partiality or hypocrisy in it. Peacemakers, when they work for peace, sow the seeds which bear fruit in holiness. This is the word of the Lord. **Thanks be to God.**

All stand to greet the Gospel. If this Acclamation is not sung it may be omitted.
Alleluia, alleluia! Happy the peacemakers, for they shall be called the sons of God. Alleluia!

THE GOSPEL   *Matthew 5.38-48*

The Lord be with you. **And also with you.**
A reading from the holy Gospel according to Matthew. **Glory to you, Lord.**
I say this to you: offer the wicked man no resistance.
Jesus said to his disciples: 'You have learnt how it was said: Eye for eye and tooth for tooth. But I say this to you: offer the wicked man no resistance. On the contrary, if anyone hits you on the right cheek, offer him the other as well; if a man takes you

to law and would have your tunic, let him have your cloak as well. And if anyone orders you to go one mile, go two miles with him. Give to anyone who asks, and if anyone wants to borrow, do not turn away.

'You have learnt how it was said: You must love your neighbour and hate your enemy. But I say this to you: love your enemies and pray for those who persecute you; in this way you will be sons of your Father in heaven, for he causes his sun to rise on bad men as well as good, and his rain to fall on honest and dishonest men alike. For if you love those who love you, what right have you to claim any credit? Even the tax collectors do as much, do they not? And if you save your greetings for your brothers, are you doing anything exceptional? Even the pagans do as much, do they not? You must therefore be perfect just as your heavenly Father is perfect.' This is the Gospel of the Lord. **Praise to you, Lord Jesus Christ.**

The Homily may follow, then Turn to page 6 for the Creed.

PRAYER OVER THE GIFTS

Lord,
may the saving sacrifice of your Son, our
  King and peacemaker,
which we offer through these sacramental signs of unity and peace,
bring harmony and concord to all your
  children.

Turn to page 8 for the Preface

Lord, under these sacramental signs of peace and unity, we offer to you the redeeming sacrifice of your Son, the King of Peace. Grant that it may strengthen the brotherhood of all your children.

COMMUNION ANTIPHON

Happy the peacemakers; they shall be called the sons of God.

Blessed are the peace-makers for they shall be called the children of God.

PRAYER AFTER COMMUNION

Lord,
you give us the body and blood of your
  Son
and renew our strength.
Fill us with the spirit of love
that we may work effectively to establish
  among men
Christ's farewell gift of peace.

Pour out on us, Lord, we pray, the spirit of charity, so that in the strength of your Son's Body and Blood, we may extend among all men the peace which he bequeathed to us: he who lives and reigns for ever and ever.

Turn to page 25 for the Concluding Rite